Sanchita

SELECTED POEMS AND LYRICS
OF POET KAZI NAZRUL ISLAM

outskirtspress
DENVER, COLORADO

The opinions expressed in this manuscript are solely the opinions of the author and do not represent the opinions or thoughts of the publisher. The author has represented and warranted full ownership and/or legal right to publish all the materials in this book.

Sanchita
Selected Poems and Lyrics of Poet Kazi Nazrul Islam
All Rights Reserved.
Copyright © 2015 Mustofa Munir
v2.0 r1.0

Cover Photo © 2015 thinkstockphotos.com. All rights reserved - used with permission.

This book may not be reproduced, transmitted, or stored in whole or in part by any means, including graphic, electronic, or mechanical without the express written consent of the publisher except in the case of brief quotations embodied in critical articles and reviews.

Outskirts Press, Inc.
http://www.outskirtspress.com

ISBN: 978-1-4787-5573-9

Outskirts Press and the "OP" logo are trademarks belonging to Outskirts Press, Inc.

PRINTED IN THE UNITED STATES OF AMERICA

Message from Poet's grand daughter

Poet Kazi Nazrul Islam always felt the pain of the ordinary people of the society where he lived and expressed that pain in the poems, lyrics, short stories, novels and dramas that he wrote.

In his life all along he upheld the doctrine of equality and unity for all people. At the confluence of his philosophy the streams of humanity, equality and unity met with great force. Poet Nazrul will remain always in our heart as a great poet, humanist and musician. He was like a moon in the night sky, a blazing sun of the day. His soul was pure, heart was broad and he never compromised with the people who had narrow, rigid view about the way the world should be.

He set an example of religious harmony and unity in his own life, in his literature and songs.

Poet Nazrul had a vision on religious harmony that he expressed in an editorial of the daily Joog Bani (Message of the Age), in 1920—

"Come O brother Hindu! Come Muslim! Come Buddhist! Come Christian! Let us transcend all barriers, forsake forever all smallness, all lies, and selfishness. Let us call brothers as brothers. We shall quarrel no more".

He assailed fanaticism and bigotry that still exist in the cauldron of society of Hindus and Muslims in Indian subcontinent amid communal strife, poverty and illiteracy. Human dignity, religious harmony, truth, beauty, pain and love were manifested continually in his resourceful poems and lyrics. The world will know more about the elegance and brilliance of his classic literary works when those works will be translated into English and other foreign languages and published thereafter. As translations of literary texts into other languages go, the tinkling of those prose and poetry never fades out rather it resonates more powerfully on readers' mind. We must ignore the ignorant people of the fanatic society and expand our relentless effort to explore his classic literature and promote his melodious songs of ragas through literary and musical conference, seminars, online and print publications worldwide.

My grandfather Poet Kazi Nazrul Islam is my inspiration, my soul, my life. Time has come to present the Poet to the young generation of this century and to the generations of many more coming centuries as a great philosopher, world-poet and musician.

For the first time ever 'Sanchita', authored by Poet Kazi Nazrul Islam, has been translated into English and published in USA.

I offer my heartfelt thanks and extend my congratulation to Professor Mustofa Munir of Virginia who translated 'Sanchita' and published it in USA. He is a poet and a fervid lover of Kazi Nazrul's literary works and songs. He has devoted himself to translate Poet's other works of poetry, novels, short stories and lyrics into English.

I want to share my moments of happiness today with

everyone who loves Poet Kazi Nazrul Islam, his poems and songs and wants those works to be spread all over the world.

Khil Khil Kazi

Contents

PREFACE xiii
BIOGRAPHY xvii

POEMS

Rebel 3
For The Joy Of Creation 10
The Devotee (Pujarini) 13
The Stoic Wayfarer 29
An Untimely Call 31
The Curse 36
The Call From The Back 40
The Victorious 42
The Thorn of Lotus 43
The Poet's Queen 44
Paush (The winter month)..................................45
Breeze Of Spring...46
The Arrow-struck Bird 51
The Fleeing Water Bird 53
The Eternal Baby..55
At The Time Of Farewell 56
A Distant Friend...58
The Evening Star 59
The Pain Of The Deep Night 60
Hope 61
Thirsty For One's Own Self 62

Today Frenzi'd Is My Mind-Bee	63
Beware, O The Helmsman!	65
Song Of The Students	67
My All-enduring Mother	69
A Struggling Poor Man	71
The Song Of Equality I Sing	73
The Creator	75
The Mankind	77
Sin	81
The Whore	85
The Woman	87
Cooli	91
A Complaint to God	94
My Explanation	99
The Graceful Young Man	104
The Ambidextrous (The Arjuna)	109
A Woman Prisoner In A Remote Island	112
The True-Poet	115
The Departing Song Of The Truthful	121
The Song of Universal Solidarity	123
The Harbinger	124
The Battle Between Hindu-Muslim	126
The Sea	129
The Sea	133
The Sea	137
My Secret Lover	140
My Lover Without A Name	144

In remembrance of a parting time	148
Poverty	150
*Falguni	155
Welcoming A Bride	158
The Bond Of Friendship	160
In a Moon-lit Night	163
The Solace	165
When The Indra Descends	167
The King-Beggar	176
The Gift Of Autumn	178
*Mrs. M. Rahman	181
Eid Mubarok	187
Who Wants To Go To Heaven	190
The Persian New Year's Day	193
The Front-travelers	197
The Immortal Zoglul*	204
A Timid Lover	211
A Row Of Betel-nut Trees By My Window	215
A Wayfarer	219
Behind The Song	223
'Tis My Pride	225
The Departure Of Monsoon	229
I Sing The Song Of Praise	231
I Sing The Hymn For Those	233
March Ahead	235
The Wave Of The Youth	237
The Blind God Of The Nativeland	241

Luffa flower 243
A Little Girl And A Squirrel 245
The Snub-Nosed Grandpa 247
The Song of Dawn 249
The Litchi Thief 251

LYRICS

[1] O Parul, Art Thou Awake? 255
[2] O Nightingale, Swing Not
    The Flower-Branch 256
[3]. You Call'd Me With An Eye-Beckon 257
[4] Sitting In Seclusion 259
[5] How Can I Forget..261
[6] My Heart Cries 263
[7] In Tender Breeze, In Shadow
    Of A Bokul Tree..264
[8] O The Stranger, Forest-Stoic 266
[9] On Which Bank Of My Life
    The Boat is Moor'd Today 268
10] Who Are You O The Charming 269
[11] Someone Forgets Not 270
[12] O My Deep River......................................271
[13] On My Broken Boat 272
[14] In Our Next Life 273
[15] The Pact 274
[16] The Reliance On The Graceful Feet 277
[17] Wash The Body Of The Cow 280

[18] In A Dawn Of Creation 283
[19] O the Young Lover 284

GLOSSARY 287

PREFACE

Poet Kazi Nazrul Islam is the author of 'Sanchita'. He selected some of his best poems and lyrics and compiled them together. He named this compiled volume of selected works as 'Sanchita' and dedicated it to Poet Rabindranath Tagore. It was first published on 2nd October, 1928 by Burman Publishing House, Kolkata, India.

As I feel, the message of his poems and lyrics in 'Sanchita' fairly deserve to be transported to the readers beyond the borders of Bangladesh and India ~ to Europe, North America, Latin America and other parts of the world since they carry the pivotal themes of love and humanity. It is my desire to let the world have a glimpse on Nazrul's extraordinary poetic genius and the beauteous heights it produced. The careful judgement on the works of Poet Nazrul will not cease until human civilization ends. Poet Nazrul has won the hearts and minds of millions of readers and fans by his poetic fineness and artistry, by his services to literature, music and the humanity.

Poet Kazi Nazrul Islam left his fans and readers in utter deprivation when he was afflicted with an unknown disease all on a sudden at the age of forty three (9th July 1942). That disease ceased his power of speech and caused him to suffer from an intense memory loss. He lost his touch with the totality of the universe around him. He was like a reticent saint in meditation. His silent ascetic life ended in August 29,1976.

In Bangladesh 'Sanchita' was first published in 1972 by

Mowla Brothers, 39 Banglabazar, Dhaka and later in 2005 by Nazrul Institute, Dhaka, Bangladesh. This book—

'Sanchita' appeared to me as the best piece of Nazrul's literary works for translation. The book contains seventy eight poems and nineteen lyrics. His famous poems ' The Rebel' (Bidrohee), 'The Proclaimer of Equality' (Shamyabadi), 'The Mankind', 'Woman', ' Devotee' (Pujarini) and 'For the joy of creation' have taken their place in 'Sanchita' gorgeously.

It took me about seven months to complete the entire translation works. I read many books on Poet Kazi Nazrul Islam's life and works. All along I kept in my mind: shall I be able to be on the same track of feelings and emotion the Poet had expressed in his poems and songs while transforming them into another language with as much less deviation as possible? Keeping that in my mind I tried to convey the Poet's core poetic message, his poetic artistry carefully in each translated poem and song of the book. I was mindful not to affect his original works in their entirety, harmony and uniformity.

I resigned myself to the impulse of the feelings that Poet felt; this impulse determined Poet's highest style that he postulated in his poetry and lyrics.

I came across many words in the poems and songs in Sanchita tough enough to be replaced by English near substitutes. As regard to the feelings, emotion and mood, Bangla language exhibits its unique manifestation. As for example, there is no lone word in English that can precisely replace some Bangla words—such as 'Aviman' or 'Avimanini' or 'Ovisharini' or 'Shuroshi'. The deep approach that we find in the tone of those Bangla words is very much lacking in their English substitutes.

I did not make any attempt to modify or alter the Persian and Arabic words; names of historic figures and places of Indian sub-continent and beyond; local names of flowers, fruits, birds and rivers of Bangladesh; names of deities and other characters in Hindu and Greek mythologies; different names of Indian musical modes and instruments; names of the outfits of Bangladeshi and Indian men and women the Poet had used in his poems and songs as those words are the basic components taken from the environment, culture, religion and people of Indian sub-continent. I left the elaborate meaning of the words printed in italic in the glossary chapter and my own words as footnotes on each poem. The information given is intented to be useful and suggestive to all readers.

I believe this translated version of 'Sanchita' will be welcomed by the students who are engaged in research in various fields of Nazrul's literary works and studying literature in colleges and universities. Much of the space of Nazrul's poetry and lyrics in this book are filled with romantic themes and inner inspiration that evolved from his young romantic heart.

The high theme and flairs of creativity that we find in Nazrul's poetry could be scaled on a par with those classic poems of Poet W. Wordsworth, John Keats, Shelly, Robert Frost, T.S. Eliot, Walt Whitman and other famous poets of the world. His poems and lyrics are embellished with words like graceful flowers bloomed with elegance that beautifies any literature. His poetry, with great theme and artistic sensitivity, validated the philosophy of human values and social justice. Poets and readers around the world will find the flavor of a classic literature and feel the superbness of poetic excellence in every page of 'Sanchita'— the masterpiece of literature.

BIOGRAPHY
Kazi Nazrul Islam (1899-1976)

"Even though I was born in this country (Bengal), in this society, I don't belong to just this country, this society. I belong to the world." - Kazi Nazrul Islam

Kazi Nazrul Islam was a poet of rebellion, love and humanity. The genius Nazrul left the imprints of his talent both on music and literature equally. His versatility was outstanding—he was a poet, short-story writer, novelist, essayist, play writer, dramatist, singer, musician, lyricist, composer, director, an actor, an activist, journalist, an editor, a soldier, a humanist and a philosopher. He was born on 25th May, 1899(BS 1306, 11th Jaistya) at Churulia of Burdwan in West Bengal, India. After the death of his father Nazrul was left in utter distress and hardship. He was nicknamed as 'dukhu mia' (The grief-stricken boy) by the village people for his battle with poverty in the childhood. Even though his profound contribution to songs, music and literature rocketed him to the peak of fame in India, the pain of poverty was still hurting him. He embraced the poverty with extreme gratefulness. Even though he encountered serious setbacks all through his life while fighting with poverty, he never failed to content us with the gifts of his music and literature.

When we read the lines below we find there a courageous Nazrul who embraced his hardship quietly as if he was an ocean that engulfed every stream of water of the earth flowing down into it. He was much obliged to indigence and hardship he faced. He wrote:

"O poverty, thou hast made me great!
Christ's honour thou hast bestow'd
On me, adorn'd me with crown
Of thorns!—
O the ascetic, an appalling courage thou hast
Given me to speak out unhesitatingly, an insolent
Nak'd look, razor-sharp words..."

Poet's all desires in life had suffered much strain and turned pale as he was stricken by the unrelenting poverty but he did not fail to compare his desire with a white shefali to be bloomed with fragrance...

"Like a white shefali my painful pallid desire wants
To bloom with fragrance spreadeth around..." [Poverty]

Nazrul wrote many lyrics and poems when he was ten years old for the plays of a theatrical group (Leto) he worked for. He learned a lot of Bengali and Sanskrit literature and Hindu scriptures when he was at that age. A year later he left the group and took admission in a high school in a town nearby his village in the year 1911. Being unable to pay school's tuition fees he frequently quit schools and got himself admitted into again. But he continued his schooling upto class X (Tenth grade) through extreme hardship.

Instead of preparing himself for the Pre-Test to qualify for the final Entrance Examination in the school, he joined the Army (49th Bengal Regiment) in the year 1917. He left the Army after two and half years as a Havildar (a non-commissioned officer) in the Regiment.

'Baunduler Atmakahini'(Autobiography of a Vagabond), his first prose work was published in May 1919 in Shougat. His poem 'Mukti'(Freedom) was published in July 1919 by the 'Bangla Mussalman Sahitya Patrika'(Bengali Muslim Literary Journal).

Poet Nazrul published his collections of short stories entitled 'Byathar Dan' (The gift of pain) in 1922 and his famous 'Agnibina' (The Vina that burns in flames)—his first anthology of poems in the same year.

He worked as a journalist for local news papers and edited many Bengali news papers in Calcutta at the same time. In 1940, he was appointed as the Chief Editor of the daily newspaper 'Nabayug' (New Age) by an eminent Bengali politician A. K. Fazlul Huq. He continued writing poetry, songs, stories, plays and dramas. His advent as a singer, play writer, actor and director in the films and theatres stirred the entire Bengal (Bangladesh and West Bengal, India) at that time. He wrote more than four thousand songs. He should be regarded as the finest lyric poet in Bengali language. He created many new ragas (musical modes) in music while he was composing his own songs known as Nazrul Geeti. The talent of Kazi Nazrul in music and literature flowed in every nook and corner of the society of common people and elites of Bengal and spread all over India within a short period of time. The poem 'Bidrohee' (The Rebel) of Kazi Nazrul was published in the 'Bijli' (The Thunder) Magazine in 1922. He reached the peak of fame immediately after the publication of that poem. Nazrul was 22 years old when he wrote this poem. The poem is considered as one of the most remarkable masterpieces of literature. The rebelliousness that exists in the theme and language of the poem encouraged both the common people and elites of India to stand against the oppression of British colonialism. The romantic poet kazi Nazrul Islam wrote many love songs and poems during his active poetic life.

Nazrul expressed strongly his view on women's equality in the society and their importance in the society along with men. In his poem 'Nari' (The Woman), he wrote:

"The song of equality I sing –
See I not any difference between man and woman!
All deeds great and e'er-beneficial were done
In this world, half of them was accomplish'd by woman,
The rest half by the man."

He explored the philosophy of Islam and Hinduism through his poetry and lyrics. He wrote and composed many Hindu devotional songs—like bhojans, kirtans and shyama songs. We do not see Poet Rabindranath Tagore wrote any devotional lyric on Islamic theme or composed any of his songs with the melody of gazal or rich devotional sufi music. Kazi Nazrul Islam abhorred fanaticism in every form that existed in the society of Muslims and Hindus in India. His philosophy was to hold the people in one great union of humanity. The introduction of the Persian and Arabic words, characters of Hindu and Greek mythology in the poems, and the style in writing poems and lyrics made him the patron saint of a new literary movement. He is still regarded for his concept of secularism and as a pioneer of a cultural renaissance in Indian literature and music.

Poet Kazi Nazrul Islam remained silent till his death.. his creation of music and literature stopped as sharply as it had begun. He left us in a void arena that is yet to be filled up. As if he knew his destiny... he wrote:

"When about thee I think
Tears roll down my cheek,
O the bless'd poet,
The sanctifying! In such a time thou hast left
Us when India needs hundreds like thee, the heat
Of the scorching sun, a burning comet thou wert!.. "[True Poet]

As an honorable citizen and the National Poet of Bangladesh he died in Dhaka on August 29, 1976 at the age of 77. He was buried in a garden-lawn and in close proximity to the mosque of Dhaka University, Bangladesh. In a song he expressed his desire to be buried nearby a mosque:

"Bury me nearby the mosque O brother!
So that I can hear the call of prayer
Of a muezzin while I'm in the grave there..."

POEMS

Rebel

Say, valiant—
Say, I hold high my head!
Bows down that peak of Himalaya when it beholds my head!
Say, valiant—
Say, slashing through the mighty sky of the mighty universe,
Passing beyond the moon, sun, planets and stars,
Penetrating the earth, orbits and heaven,
Severing the throne of the god, I've risen-
I'm the eternal wonder of the god of universe!
On my forehead the enrag'd god glares,
The lustrous royal insignia of goddess
Of victory dazzles!
Say, valiant—
I'm the eternal lofty head!

I'm impolite, ferocious, ungovernable ever,
On the day of cataclysm I'm the best dancer,
I'm the cyclone, the destruction! The curse of the world, fear terrible!
Everything I break to pieces! Irresistible,
Unruly, unregulat'd I'm; all bindings, rules, discipline I trample!
A restive, I capsize load'd boat, I'm torpedo, a floating mine dreadful!
I'm *Dhurjati*, an untimely summer windy storm violent!
I'm a rebel, the rebel-son of the god of the whole world!
Say, valiant—
I hold high for-ever my head!

Whatever on my way I find I break! I'm the cyclone, the storm,
On my own beat I dance, I'm a dance-crazy rhythm!
I'm the unfetter'd joy of life, I'm joyful!
I'm *Hambira*, *Chayanaut*, *Hindol*,
A restless, with pomp and glamour instantly I startle!
While on the street I jump and dangle!
I'm agitat'd, an unsteady swing ever!
I do whatever I want, whenever!
With death I engage in arm-wrestling,
To enemy I extend my charming
Friendship, I'm a storm, a lunatic!
To the world I'm a dread, an epidemic;
I'm the rule, the panic, the slaying,
The heat, the ever-impatient dismaying!
Say, valiant–
I'm the eternal lofty head!

A forever defiant, intoxicat'd, invincible I'm! Always,
Always with wine my dearest cup overflows!
I'm the flame of sacrificial fire; that fire I maintain,
I'm the sage *Jamadagni*, the priest, the fire, an oblation,
The creation, destruction, crematorium, a human habitation,
I'm the end of a night– I'm the end!
On my forehead is the sun,
With moon in hand I'm *Indrani's* son,
In my one hand a curv'd bamboo flute,
In the other I hold a trumpet!
Churn'd poison I drank,
I'm *Krishna's* throat, the ocean of pain!
I'm *Byomkesh*, I seize the

Wanton flow of *Gangotri*,
Say, valiant—
I hold high for-ever my head!

I'm an ascetic, a melody-soldier,
I'm the prince, fad'd out is my ochreous royal attire!
I'm Bedouin, I'm Genghis, to none
    I bow down
    But to me! I'm the sound
In the north-eastern horn,
I'm a thunder,
In the bugle of *Israfil* I'm the terrifying roar!
I'm *Pinak-pani*'s drum, spear three-prong'd,
The rod of *Dharmaraj*, spinning wheel and conch,
I'm the dreadful sound
Of the mystic syllable–Om!
I'm angry *Durbasha*, disciple of *Vishwamitra*, the heat of wild fire,
I'll burn the universe! I'm an ecstasy, a lively candid laughter—
A great terror, hostile to the creation,
I'm the eclipse of the doomsday's twelfth sun!
Sometime I'm quiet, sometime agitat'd, despotic extremely,
I'm the youth of the crimson morning sun, humbling to destiny!
I'm violent ocean-waves, tempest's ferocity, I'm bright, shining,
Rippling of water, swinging of waves moving!

I'm the fire in the eyes of a belle, a braid of an unrestrain'd virgin,
I'm oblig'd, an impetuous love in the lotus-heart of a teen,

I'm a distract'd mind of a stoic, a widow's sobbing,
Dismay and anger of the dismay'd, wayfarer's pain depriving,
I'm a perpetual homeless traveler; the heart-grief of a humiliat'd,
Torment of poison, an impetus anew in the heart of a disgrac'd belov'd!
I'm the deep intimate pain, the grumbling of a resentful-ever-agitat'd heart,
I'm the trembling first touch of a virgin, her... shivering in a furtive kiss!
I'm a timid glance of an esoteric lover, her every moment of deceitful gaze!
I'm the love of a wanton girl,
The jingling of her conch bangles.

I'm an eternal baby, an e'er-juvenile,
I'm conceal'd modesty-vest of a youth-fearful village belle!
I'm the northern wind, gentle breeze vernal,
The eastern stoical gust, I'm deep musical
Mode of a wayfarer-poet,
In a bamboo-*vina* I'm that song play'd!
I'm an extremely heat-afflict'd thirst, the sun infuriat'd,
A desert and a cascade,
I'm a pleasant green shadowy portrait!
Being engross'd in happiness of spiritual trance I run,
What a lunatic I'm, I'm an insane!
From all fetters I'm free, suddenly myself I've known!

I'm the rise, the fall, the consciousness of the unconscious,
I'm the banner at the gate of the universe,
The victorious flag of mankind.

Like a storm I clap and run,
In my control the earth and heaven,
The *borrak* and *uccaisraba* are my own
Vehicles with mighty neighing they run!
I'm the the volcano, the annihilating wild fire,
I'm the blaze under the sea, the drunken flare
Beneath the earth, I'm uproarious, tumultuous sea, murmuring!
On the lightning I mount and fly with strong snapping,
I arouse terror in the earth, earthquake I create suddenly!
I grip the hood of the snake-king abruptly,—
The fire-wing of the angel Gabriel I grab violently!
I'm a divine baby, wanton, audacious,
With my teeth I tear off the *anchal* of mother-universe!

The vast restless sea, I 'm the flute of *Orpheus*,
With my slumberous kiss I silence the whole universe,
The melodious *pashori* is in my flute
And I'm the *Shyam's* flute.
I'm enrag'd when the endless sky I traverse,
In fear the fire of the terrible hell slowly extinguishes with flickers!
I'm the rebellious army in the whole universe!

I'm the monsoon, deluge and flood,
Sometimes I welcome this earth,
Sometimes I'm terribly destructive and oblig'd—
Twin daughters I'll snatch from *Vishnu's* chest,
I'm injustice, meteors, saturn, the blaze of comet,
I'm the decapitat'd *chandi*, cobra venomous!
A war-monger ruinous!
While sitting there on the hell fire I smile

The flowery smile!

I'm clay-built, I'm supreme, ageless, immortal, imperishable,
I'm the fear of mankind, a demon and god, e'er-invincible,
I'm the lord, the supreme man, the truth!
Wantonly I roam all o'er the heavens, earth and beneath the earth!
I'm an insane! I'm an insane!!
I've known myself, today I'm free from all obstacles and chain!

I'm the cruel axe of *Parsurama*, all warriors
From the earth I'll exterminate, peace
I'll bring tranquility magnanimous!
On the shoulder of *Balarama* I'm the plough, with negligence
I'll uproot the subservient universe amid happiness
Of new creation! That day I'll be quiet—
The rebel, battle-weari'd!
When wailing and outcry of the oppress'd
In the air and sky will not be echo'd,
When the clanking of the tyrant's sword
Will no more resonate across the dreadful battle-field—
That day I'll be quiet
O the rebel, battle-weari'd!

I'm the rebel *Bhrigu*, on the bosom of god my footprint
I leave, I'm the creator of slaying, I'll rip off the chest
Of the destiny capricious afflict'd with pain
And grief! I'm the *Bhrigu* rebellious, on
The bosom of god my footprint I'll leave!
The chest of the whimsical destiny I 'll rip!

I'm the perpetual rebel valiant—
Towering o'er the universe alone I stand,
I'm the eternal lofty head!
[Agni-bina]

A few words:

Poet wrote this poem in the year 1921 while he was in Calcutta, India. The whole poem is adorned with an iconoclastic theme the poet brought in to instill an awakening spirit and consciousness in the heart of the people of undivided India who were subjugated and victims of injustice and oppression under the British colonial government. The poet delivered his message that stands against all kinds of subjugation, injustice and oppression exist in the human world. In the poem he displayed the strength of character, sturdiness of will, a keen intellect and thoughts with powerful conviction and ethical courage. The poet is that "I'm" who is someone or something in its extreme form — like a volcano, tempest, cyclone, deluge, fire, sun, saturn and cataclysm. He is the one who can smile while sitting on the hell-fire. At one time he is indomitable, an angry god and sage, the other time he is an impetuous love, an ascetic and a melody-soldier. His softness of feelings is like the feelings of the first touch and shivering kiss of a virgin girl. He is like a gentle vernal breeze, a bamboo flute and musical modes. I see Poet's radiant expression is beaming from this poem like the beam of the glorious morning sun on the highest peaks of the mighty Himalaya.

For The Joy Of Creation

Today I'm ecstatic for the joy of creation!

My face laughs,
My eyes laugh,
My blood laughs seethingly!
Today I'm ecstatic for the joy of creation!

Today in my little pool of confined life rises
A deluging tide with high crushing waves!
Comes there the smile and lamentation,
Freedom and restriction,
Today I speak out,
My chest bursts out,
From my bitter sorrows
Happiness emanates!
From my indigent bosom emerges the pain!
Today I'm ecstatic for the joy of creation!

Today the apathy grows, dismay is exhal'd,
A chest-rending sigh heaves out,
The enraged sea is billowing, dangles
The sky and the wind blows!
In the sky the *chakra* spins,
With his trident appears the ruinous
God! Comets and meteors want the destruction
Of creation, that I behold today and
In my heart smile the flowers of million gardens,
Today I'm ecstatic for the joy of creation!

Today the fire smiles,

The spring breathes,
Arrows stain'd with blood
Are thrown by the god of love, overwhelm'd
Are *polash, ashok* and *shimul* !
In the horizon spreads there the spectrum colorful,
Oh! All over *digbalika's* yellow-apparel
That vividness shimmers!
Today in my invigorat'd courtyard there comes
All around me the vernal coloration!
Today I'm ecstatic for the joy of creation!

Today in deceitful indignation an arrow I hold,
There they come—all maidens alluring! Red
Is someone's foot like blood-shiny bosom's skin,
Someone with beauty dazzling,
Someone looks sad with tears in her eyes!
Nearby me lies the *vina* of their untold words,
Their tale I'll tell, in my eyes tears melt down,
Today I'm ecstatic for the joy of creation!

Today there comes the dawn,
Evening and noon,
The near, the far; there resonates an unrestraint
Frenzi'd-rhythm in a frantic passionate outburst!
In flaccid *shiuli* the autumn emerges,
Smiles of dew on the blades of grasses!
Today I'm ecstatic for the joy of creation!

Today the sea rises, desert smiles,
Tremble the earth, forest and trees!
There comes the earth-drowning storm with swelling
Upstream, in the wind songs of *bhairavis* drift along,

On my right—lies a new-born child,
On my left—a dead old decrepit!
O like an unbound horse my mind runs,
Wild it becomes!
Today I'm ecstatic for the joy of creation!
Today I'm ecstatic for the joy of creation!!

A few words:
The thrilling emotion that emanates from the heart of a poet who is overwhelmed with the joy and happiness of creation is manifested in each line of this poem. What else can give a poet immense pleasure other than creating his poem that evolves from his heart? Much of that joy spills over his heart when he is admired and recognized by someone or by the people around him for his poetic achievement. When Nobel laureate Poet Rabindranath Tagore dedicated his musical drama 'Bashanta' to Poet Nazrul, he was very delighted to receive a book dedicated to him. That happiness inspired him to write the above poem when he was in the prison cell. Amid the bitterness of sorrows and dismay the flowers of million gardens smiled in his heart. He was so thrilled as if his mind was like a wild horse without rein, like high crushing sea waves, like the dew that smiles on the blades of grasses.

The Devotee (Pujarini)

After so many days at this inopportune
Time— when I dance
Day and night
In the bloody mortal-sport
Like a dust-blinding whirlwind—
O my beloved!
After so many days I doth know
At this inopportune time — through
Generations I know thee!
O the devotee!
That melodic musical mode, that voice,
The eyes, eyebrows, forehead, cheek and face,
Thy phenomenal beauty, thy dangling,
Like a victorious she-swan thy dance-faulty swinging!
I know, I know everything!

On a frustrat'd, wearied, dried up, burnt
Beach of life myself in a swoon I found,
So from my deep heart
I call'd thee O my belov'd!
Thy sweetest name I cherish and utter silently!
In a torn voice I cry out,— I know, I know thee!
Neither art thou a victorious nor a mendicant,
A goddess, a chaste, an ascetic virgin,
My devotee thou art!
Through ages lovest thou this brute!
Thyself burnest thou whilst kindling a lamp in my heart,
Time and again thy devotion made me indebt'd!
My sweet heart I've known thee for many generations!
At the setting hour of my life I know thee often times,

After we're known,
Alone in an unknown
Land I'm without thee,
In an empty parting-raft thou hadst left me!...

Sitting in the twilight of the day in tearful
Eyes the past memories I recall —
At the end of spring with fading hope that
Night my silent arrival, my eyes met
Thy eyes, became delightful!-
My youth was yet to bloom, happy and simple!
Longing eagerly with pain
I came like a dawn,
Half sleepy, half awaken'd,
Still in my adolescence
The colorful day-break of my life spread
Not yet; unhinder'd wanton dance of whirling wind,
Indomitable force of songs and laughter I brought,
A lost traveler I'm from a far distant land!
At night I arriv'd with a pain of a wandering lost man–
Woke up in the morning,
Awakening melody I sang –
Thou hadst woken up— sat by me,
Smil'd at me pallidly— a pain I felt in me
When I saw thine ambient smile-- I ask'd thee—
'Alone in wilderness whose tame bird art thou?'
What an appealing look 'twas in thine eyes I saw!
Then I perceiv'd— thou art that melody of mine— that
Forest-swinging melody with pain of estrangement;
That flowers-blooming melody in southern breeze;
That melody entices a deer in wilderness!
Since my primordial birthday thou dost know me,

O thou dost know me!
Then—in a fit of pique a parting song
At the midnight hours I sang,
My heart with pain fills, I know not yet
Whom I want'd to contain in my bereav'd heart
On the pretext of singing a song! Though
Only I know —
Amaz'd me thine sleepy bashful eyes!
One more thing in thine eyes I saw — a surprise,
A sparkling lustrous thrill, a deep pain of love melt'd
There, in pity the estrang'd
Lover like a dark cold night shiver'd!

So pleasing 'twas
To my thirsty eyes
O *Pujarini*! Thy kindl'd eye-lamp emitt'd
Cool-compassionate light!

Then—I sang
A song,
With a smile perhaps I call'd thee
By thy name to sit by me,
Dangl'd up at once thine calm eyes
That shed tears like a cascade from the source
Of pain with a roaring resentment (why, who knows),
That much tears, little-bit of caress
Bred so much resentment!
O the neglect'd,
O my mendicant devotee!
Tell me, tell me!

On my broken bosom keeping thy weeping face,

Tell me, O tell me—feelest thou sadness
When thou beholdest me?
Thine eyes get tearful if I call thee?
An unknown, unfamiliar traveler I'm, why tears
Dropeth from that girl's eyes?
Everyone laughs at me, my scalding-curs'd-breath
Burns my built-home,
Considering me a jewel many keep me around their necks,
When a snake it becomes and inflicts
A venomous bite on someone's chest,
Tramples he instantly the snake under his foot!
So much the world hates him, what a cruel game thou playest
With him? O the vagrant!
Harbor so much resentment?
Somehow a right he had to call thee by name,
That inflicts thee with pain?
No one ever lov'd thee?
No one ever caress'd thee?
Thou art a born vagrant?
So much tears in thy eyes, grief and compassion!

No, that's not true—
'No, that's not true!'—
Which resentful one says that from his heart?
Many men came to thee, insatiate,
Hungry thou art for love and affection!
Why thy love spills over when
Thou dost see me?
My queen, that's a mystery!
No one knows— knowest thou not—
I know not though!

Only my love and heart doth know—
Wherefrom that pain of fascination
Grows in the our hearts for no reason?...

That day I realiz'd—O the unknown!
To me thou art ever known,
Through ages thou art my *Shita* disdain'd!
Thou dost make the forest weeping,
O the ascetic-girl, the chaste, ever virgin!
Many times thy tray I broke filled with offerings,
For a plea of game I tore thy garland;
O the ever-reticent,
The cursed goddess!
Everything quietly thou hast
Condon'd- O the devotee,
Instincts prompt'd thee,
With ease thou hast persuad'd,
Thou art my goddess of victory, I'm thy Poet!

Then, in deep night I sat by thee, listen'd to thy songs —
A kind of nervous, engross'd thou wert in shyness!
In thy song's melody a lost voice I trac'd—
In my mind it flash'd
Back and fad'd away again! As if it says,
'O belov'd, thou dost know me through ages!'
Shyam forgot his *Radhika*, *Radhika* wept in wilderness,
As if 'twere a bewailing of remote sadness,
Torments of negligence!
Forsaken by her husband lonely *Dayamanti* wander'd around
In forest, with the same fatigu'd voice she call'd
Him, lonely *Shakuntala* in the forest secretly wept.

Hem was in the peaks of mountain, by being *Uma* she
   return'd –
The abandon'd call'd *Bholanath* with anguish'd
Tone, for her husband she wept!
I'm aware of, I perceive all those—
'Twas my youth not yet bloom'd, thy image
Touch'd not my heart deeply! Nonetheless, my song
I left in thy voice that I knew and head'd for an unknown
Distant land! What a surprise! So soon
Cri'd out my phenomenal pain
With musk-fragrance, at the bank of the sacred
Gumoti, at the lotus-feet!

Where's the source of the pain-laden
Intoxicating fragrance—
I want to know, my warm deep sigh creat'd tremor
In the sky, land and earth! The creepers, leaves, flowers,
Birds and rivers, the clouds and wind, all weep relentlessly,
The unappeas'd god with fervent of youth cries euphorically!
Ill-fat'd life wander'd around and cried—
Where's my love?' In profound dejection cries the heart,
Mind becometh stoical! As though
This world is a blight'd youth, a lover's painful dismay!
In red and blue in the eyes float many colorful shadows,
They come and come—why that intoxicating musk's
Fragrance doth want to come into my heart?
There runs my mind-deer, in fear horizon trembles for my
   enrag'd
Wailing! Like musk deer my fragrance-addict'd
Mind-deer looketh for my own fragrance!
My own love doth want to quench
The thirst of its own desire! With unending thirst

Of *Agastya* my youth till its drop last
Wants to drink the ocean endless!
O god, O god! Immense thirst boundless!
Where's that satiety? My thirst-allaying
Sea of love –the sea unending?

Where can I find someone more turbulent,
More wayward and restless than I! In mind
No peace I find in this big world! I think and
Walk, there goes so many street-maidens,
Behind them goes my love-hungry mind
With a blind-speedy approach! If someone
Looks at me – in utter resentment tears
Melt in my eyes! They laugh at me! Says
Someone at the door– 'Take the alms'.
More deject'd my heart becomes,
Growls that beggar's heart in
Deep shameless pain!

Like a clamorous devastating sea the agitat'd
Flame of my life dangles, swells up in pain and
Resentment ! Street-maidens offer me alms,
On their pride I kick'd hard, it shatter'd into pieces
Along with alms! In tears they left me, scar'd
To come back again; like a helpless orphan in a food
Oblation my dedicat'd vagrant-heart begs
Alms for the love of Buddha," Give me alms
O the city people!" But the hungry walks
Away from the door without alms!

There came many women, many went back~ some with fear,
Some with surprise, some with broken-heart, some with tears

In eyes! To them I surrender'd fully! City's happy domestic
Wives understand that not. With smile they come and
 go back
To their canopies of love with tears!
They say, "O the traveler! Tell us, tell us,
What's in thy heart thou dost cherish?
The pain in thy tone! Hunger in thy heart!"
Nobody doth understand!
To me many women came with heart,
With youth, with beauty elegant!
With their riches drunken boastful rich women
Want to entrap me with their beauty in the garden
Of their youth! cries my heart in vain
On the road in utter frustration –
"Where's my mendicant *Pujarini?*"
"An ascetic I'm in loving thee,
O my Husband! I'm a destitute, thy pride,
Not a victorious though!"— Said she, in the desert
I wander, it flares up my thirst —
Meanwhile my thirsty heart had lost
The track, there someone far away
Beckon'd me! She doth weep and say—
"'Tis me, thy mendicant,
O my husband!
I know thee,
Thou knowest me!"
Her tone I recogniz'd not, a call of a witch!
False illusion! not the water 'tis
But an illusory mirage malicious!
At her door I came, begg'd, "Give me alms".
But where's my mendicant? Ah! A witch she
Is! Unscrupulous, wants to slay me!

'Tis like cruel trap of barbarous hunters,
Deviously she wants to grab my offerings,
But fail'd,
In her own trap the crafty liar died!

With thorn-prick'd blood-stain'd head when
I came to thee, I knew not then my pain
Thou hast felt! Yet many times it cross'd my mind,
Thy cold touch appeas'd my torments, my scorch'd wound.
In thy heart I felt my heart weeps always—
Thou askest : 'Tell me, tell me!' O the wayfarer! Where's
Thy pain? Quiet thou art, secret,
An ascetic, reticent,
Thy silent-perpetual words I hardly heard, hardly understood!
Hope and love had shed tears in that bosom suppress'd!

Meanwhile like an unobstruct'd stream— in a stormy night
I saw my mother, in her lap she took me, kiss'd my wet
Eyes, gone are my grief and agonies!
A mother's love like a lamp of *deayali* dangles
From a broken window! A lost mother I found as if a homeless
Man found his home; in mother' bosom after many years
I slept in peace, no more singing on the street,
Many times my street-friend in stormy night
Call'd me, with a frustrat'd sigh he left!

Perhaps once again my trail I lost—
Perhaps a victorious woman was obstruct'd at the gate!
Whom I'm looking for in the streets I've forgotten,-

My heart—the infinite tryster begg'd for which adoration,
I fail'd to recall that!
Those pain and grief I remember not,
With tears of fresh happiness
My heart melt'd down, wet were my tearless eyes,
As if eyes sank into a graceful lotus,
Bosom was fill'd with fragrance!
What a violent painful-happiness
Overflow'd my heart with ecstasy and pleasures!
Died once again the arrow-struck burglar-bird,
Temple altar stain'd with my blood all o'er, respond'd
Not the stone idol, in humiliation all my crimson-glowing
    pain
Stood up aggressively, riding the blood-horse of rebellion
I mov'd fast with rage towards
The creator of pain through clouds;
Igniting the sacrificial malic'd fire in the cataclysmic smoke
Of a comet I creat'd horror in the desert— dry and devoid
    of love!

An illusion! From afar thy *vina* calls me by my dear name!
    Looking at
The Far-off secret path my malic'd-blood-eyes get wet
With tears of pain! Recalling that tone of call my past pain
    I forgot,
I understand– thou dost exist, the truth thou art,
With whole heart thou wantest me, the forest-girl! Alone
    in a listless
Mind for me thou stringest garland with hidden shyness,
Through generations thou art my mendicant! The sea of fire
In my heart transforms into a flower,
It smiles and says, 'I know, I know thee!

Be alive, O morbid! 'Tis she who calls thee
From afar— snatch'd thy peace and happiness!'
Someone weeps there? Someone behind cri'd out—'My friend,
The time is not congruous!' But I listen'd
Not to it, bereft wailing of a charming girl
Reaches my heart since time eternal!
Breathlessly I ran unto thee, somewhere my fire-chariot
Is crush'd, burnt is the blood-flag, in my heart
Thy conceal'd devotion thus
Brought the comfort of the universe!

Words are lost what I was about to say, I've
No life, tears, hopes and strength,
Today I will sing
No song—
But some lively words of tears— blood-exud'd !
Mere civility a shameless beggar expect'd
While receiving alms! That's true, my dear, as thou thinkest!
Those memories I recall make me laugh today, my belov'd!
From door to door I walk'd, got frustrat'd,
Came back and told thee my wish last!
With all my hope and love I ador'd thee,
O my dear heartless devotee!
When the world failed to put up with me
I thought my encumbrance thou wouldst endure smilingly—
With love and negligence subdue this world-rebel.
From thy heart the light phenomenal
Would emit the pride of conquering this unexplor'd,
Unbending lover! Then, one day infusing a great
Strength into me
The rebel's goddess of victory thou wouldst be!

With hope and strength tearing apart the universe
I will bring down the offerings of torn red lotus
To thy glowing feet! But alas!
Where art thou? Where's that liveliness?
Where's the deep attraction?
That 'thou'—not anymore thou art today; I see
Treacherous thou art, with lie and treachery
Victorious thou wantest to be!
A little dost thou want to give me,
A little dost thou save for someone,
O the unfortunate one!
Seeing all these I laugh! Whom dost thou cheat?
In my heart lies always the true god, that heart
He sees vividly when He looks into someone!
My dear, pollut'd and stain'd is thine devotion,
Thou dost want to cheat
Someone whom by heart and soul thou adorest!

So I think, 'Whose fault was it!—
When the light of death was kindl'd in thy taint'd heart?
Yet I think, 'Is it true? An unscrupulous woman thou art?

If 'tis so, O the witch! O the wicked,
Let it be true. Kindle the light of falsehood!
Let's all be in falsehood—
Thou, me, the sun, the moon, the star, the planet ~
O the woman'perfidious! Kindle, kindle more light of falsehood!

While thy face I behold my shame strikes
My heart like a thunder; within me I die recalling thy loveless,

Careless manner and my shamelessness!

I feel like crying aloud, 'O my mother earth, split
Into two; take thy hate-inflict'd, dirt-smear'd
Son, his shameless face from the light
Into darkness!' With hope again I approach thee;
As I look at thy face, Oh! What I see!
Where's my *Pujarini*?
Where's my indigent holy woman?
'Tis the same old negligence!
Same e'er-emotionless face!
In disgrace my heart breaks ~
Perfect she is not, the same deception !
Ah! Such a dreadful game those crook'd women
Have play'd! With my ooz'd out blood from heart
Like tint of lac they anoint their feet!
Greedy they're, love of whole universe they want!
A lover's whole heart'd devotion and submission
They reject, seeing such devotion they're frighten'd!
Not with one they're happy,
More devotion they want from many!
Greedy mind is satisfi'd not with one,
They desire many men ...
Much I worshipp'd not my creator God
But her I worshipp'd!
In return pangs of her betrayal I receiv'd!

At the end I realiz'd, my death is nigh,
In bitter happiness my
Heart bursts into roars,
O my Mind! Here and there
For whom I weep? I flare up

Like blazing eyes of destructive *Bhairab!*
Give some claps in utter frustration!
Ignite the eternal fire, thy flame of rebellion!
Blow thy ruinous bugle-horn! Bring up thy fire-chariot,
Throw thy *porshu*-trident! Destroy this city of falsehood!
Bring the blood, ambrosia, and poison! Strangulate
The death! Let the world of falsehood
Break into pieces
By thine crushing pressure ponderous!

So much poison I swallow'd, so much burning
Today! O dear girl, I recall often~ so long
I lov'd thee not, so long I perceiv'd not
Thy conceal'd blushing light of heart,
Till that day thou hadst
Desire'd me, O my belov'd, till that
Day thou wert my mendicant,
Till that day tears dropp'd down in resentment
And repugnance, pain ripp'd thy heart
For little bit of love, for little bit of affection! Sitting
By me so many nights thou hadst spent staying
Awake, to thee I paid no attention;
Revenge thou hadst taken
For that! With false allegation and in disgrace
Thou hadst strangl'd me! O the merciless!
Today from my death-bed I cry ~ the cruelest
Game with my life thou hadst
Played! Deeply someone thou lovest,
Him how couldst thou neglect?
Such a blow only man can inflict!
I us'd to think then—
'Tis a quality of an unblemish'd virgin

To offer herself to someone she
Loveth in the twinkle of an eye!

Wrong, that's wrong! Wind makes
The flowers to bloom, bees
Cometh to molest them! Wind is valorous;
Love is not for him, my dear!
The bees know better
How to squeeze the flower-bud
And its heart!

I'm the traveler, southwardly wind,
Toward an unknown land the journey I started at the end
Of spring! The land where neither death nor night exists!
At the parting moment heart fills with happy tears,
Delight'd I'm with those memories! Thou didst love me
Before I lov'd thee,
On my bosom and face the cool light
Of love dropeth first from thy virgin heart!
The colorful deluge of excitement
And happiness touch'd my broken heart!
That pleasure I recall,
That glowing loving memory I feel,
My Life and birth are gratified!
Death I can embrace with content
Today! Before I lov'd thee,
Thou didst love me,
Today many times I kiss
On thy name with that bliss!

While recalling me, O dear, -in one night if in thy heart
Pain thou feelest while sleeping on someone's chest,

Consider this troublesome, the menace breath'd his last!
Never again none shall come to kiss on thy lotus-feet
With carnal pleasure! Dead is he, the restless, insatiate,
Ever-selfish, greedy,—
Becometh immortal—in thy love he will be
Deathless forever with torment
Of poison— the *Nilkantha*-Poet!
[Dulon-chapa]

A few words:
The romantic poet Nazrul captured the theme of poetic romanticism in this poem that readily demonstrated his feelings and emotions for his beloved lover, a devotee of his love. He gave the impression of becoming so romantic in his feelings that ran so deep while he expressed his desire to live as an immortal lover in her heart withstanding all pains and torments of estrangement by being the Nilkantha! The Poet in the guise of a romantic lover in separation and union, with the emotions both abstract and concrete wants to see her as his devotee for ever.

The Stoic Wayfarer

In a waning daylight the stoic wayfarer
Thinks, far away somewhere
He wants
To go! *The stoic wayfarer thinks!*

'Come unto home', a call came through,
Said again the evening~'No, not you'
On the road the wayfarer wanders around,
And
Knows not who's gonna shelter him!
The stoic wayfarer thinks!

With love the shadows of woods had fallen
Upon the hair of horizon
Girls, to find him at the foothills of green
The mountain girl steps down,
The stoic wayfarer thinks!

Happiness of the night the lamp brings, fear
Of hidden joy it conveys to the heart of a lover,
In a desert'd home alone she sings,
The stoic wayfarer thinks!

The trail he lost all on a sudden,
In deep darkness he is imprison'd!
At the navigating star worri'd looks he cast!
Can he find again the lost trail towards the east?
The stoic wayfarer thinks!
(Dulonchapa)

A few words:
Poet depicted him as a stoic wayfarer, a wayfarer who didn't know where to take shelter in his journey of life – who will give him shelter in the miseries and afflictions that beset him. He lost the trail. He was worried whether he would get the trail back in the journey of his life with the help of true guidance like the evening star in the sky!

An Untimely Call

Whom I loved not so much
As I want'd to, why so often comes
He in my mind now
At this unseemly time though?

Kissing on my eyes, I recall, every night he lull'd
Me to sleep, my morn sleep he disrupt'd
Many a time with kisses!
At that moment I thought, 'Isn't it too much!'
Desperately from him I want'd to flee away!
With tears the memories I recall today,
On the dust laden with pain
His pride was tumbl'd down!

That spill'd over love of a fresh heart
I trampl'd with complacence! Why that
Much attachment I feel today? My foot
He took on his bosom and kiss'd it;
Out of conceit, mother, him I ignor'd
With extreme disregard!

In his eyes torments I saw as no one show'd
Him cordiality! Driven away by everyone he need'd
Some peace I could have offer'd!
O mother, him I reject'd!
A god I recogniz'd not,
In the guise of a beggar at
My door came he the King great!

On a wrong trail unto me he came!

By being a beggar could I recognize him?
O dear mother! So I receiv'd not his offerings,
His garland of jewels! But with full offerings
The god worship'd me! In the darkness of ritual's turbid
Smoke I discern'd him not!

His last desire was to love me, O mother, that I knew not!
Left in this world only farewell message of the royal-guest.
O my love! Where had you been when my king stood at
My door-step? The world sighs with sore—
'Whom do you look for? Here he is no more!'

A wayfarer perpetual never feels an attraction for
A home! O mother, a shadowy path calls him from afar,
At the far end of the field his *nupur* in the feet jingles!
With the blooming of flowers he blooms,
With clouds he walks up the hill, he comes, he goes,
I know not really whom he adores!

That much vigor do I have to enchant a wayfarer wandering?
Neither love nor the evening-lamp call'd him in,
That's why, mother, door in my heart open'd not when
He knock'd that, perhaps someone else he lov'd then!
Him I push'd away, the offend'd,
The home-abandon'd!

With love and passion he want'd
To cuddle me, in fear his passionate love I avoid'd!
His dark eyes pleas'd me from distance, with tears
In eyes when he would come nearer to me
A tone I would miss in the cord of my heart,
In pain I would become despondent!

O mother, today like him why do I want
Passionately to get his touch, love and caress that
I neglect'd in the past! Today keeping my face on his chest
With deep happiness I want to cry for the yawning pain to put
An end to my life! My wailing reaches not his
Land of garden? Today I realiz'd my whole comfort and peace
Of this life he stole, O my King of the spring! The comforter of heart!
Come and take my garland as I conced'd defeat!
Today in groaning desolation my chest breaks apart,
O mother, come and see how much tears today I could shed!

The truth you told --the stone can
Bleed, heat of wild fire can scorch the snow-mountain!
In my bosom arous'd a severe tide!
Door it broke, in my speechless heart
There came a garrulous god
From a terrible sea! I want to talk,
In me my heart explodes,
Mother, today resist me not!

Burnt was my paradise as soon as he left,
Alone the first wedding night I spent
With bereav'd heart!
At dawn he will neither
Wake me up nor will he come in a tryst
Of stealth-kiss in deep night,
Near the forest he will wander with broken heart
In the stormy night!

O mother, if I were with him again
At his feet I would tumble down,
His feet I would wash with red lotus
In the lake of my eyes!
My *anchal* I would spread to let him sit,
His tearful eyes, his cheek, face and lips wet
With my collyrium I would wipe,
Holding him around with my hair his feet I would mop,

Keeping the face on his noble chest this feindish ruinous
Would say 'I love you'! Cheek would flush, face
Would sweat in happy-shyness,
I would slip down there
On his lap, O mother!
Then I would see—
How could he stay away from me!

Now so much hopes and love fill my heart,
Laden with resentment,
Pain, anger and affection!
To his tears I'm beholden!
To which far-off unknown island
Now he's exil'd?
Going that far denies that stormy wind?

If he knew that I loved him, his grave would
Shatter in happiness! In ecstasy he would cry out –
Suppressing tears the world-sea would shiver,
With his roaring the volcano would deliver
In rage! The earth, the sky, the wind
Would start around him whirling dance!

O mother, weep not, rather tell me something,
On your lap let me sleep while listening
To you! ~ 'Who push'd the door open? 'Tis the wind
That pushes the door open the way he used
To do!' O the wind! O the tempestuous wind!
There at the shore is your friend!

Could he come to me
Where I'm still alive!
To such a place he has gone
Where exists not my shadow even!
Yet time and again I feel to call
Him, my untold words whom I would tell?
The crying of my heart, O mother
Strikes on my bosom's door!

Good-bye O mother, tell him if you see
Him again, 'Tis the king's offering~ a beggar like me
Can he neglect? Mother, for sure I know my indignant
Lover in deep night will come back again at
The door of this hut, tell him then... in search
Of him lost I'm in the darkness!
(Dulonchapa)

A few words:
The bemoaning Poet's beloved was narrating her feelings of excruciating pain to her mother that she once neglected her beloved and failed to make a bond with him though he came to her again and again with the thirst of passion and love. Now she is repented but her lover-poet may not come back to knock her door again,... in search of him she went out in the darkness.

The Curse

That day thou wilt realize
When lost I'll be,
Thou wilt ask the evening star about me—

Carrying my picture on thy bosom thou wilt cry like an insane
And wander around in desert, forest, and mountain;
In the sky, air and ocean
Thou wilt look for me,
That day thou wilt realize!

From a dream wake up thou wilt in deep night
By a touch that thrill'd thee as if that
Touch was known to thee! Thou thinkest
I breathe nearby thee, the bed thou wilt
Find empty
When thou wantest to touch me,
That dream's not true! In pain clos'd are thine eyes!
That day thou wilt realize!

With heavy heart and sobbing thou singest,
Listeners around thee doth ask - "Isn't that
Song thou wert taught by a traveller?" Thou wilt
Feel like weeping, in thy voice that
Melodious *bihaga* will weep! Our deceitfulness thou wilt
Recall, again and again wipest
Thou thy tearless eyes,
That day thou wilt realize!

Again when *shewli* will bloom to cover thy courtyard,
When with flowers thou makest a garland

Thy bangles will shake— the courtyard
Will weep! In thy remembrance my *shewli*-cover'd
Grave will weep! Pain thou shalt feel in thy garland,
O girl, thy smile tears will take away!
Thou wilt realize that day!

Blows again the autumn breeze, dew will wet
The night, not this man nearing to death
Will be there again! A foggy night will come! Friends, kith
And kin will surround thee, warmth
Of embrace thou shalt feel at night,
The touch of thine lover's bosom will remind
Thee my touch—a distaste
Thou wilt feel, that day thou wilt realize!

There will be winter again, but he won't be there!
Thy happiness he would shatter
By being around thee, he won't be there!
That day thou wilt recall on
My arm when wouldst sleep, Ah! in aversion
Thou wouldst turn away thy face! In thy bed every
Moment that memory will prick thee ~
That day thou wilt realize!

In the river again tide will rise, boat will swing,
Someone in the boat will be that day, boat will swing.
Thou shalt remember – in one night together we were
In the boat, the same tide was there in the river,
Prevail'd there the same darkness, the boat drift'd along as
Usual *~that day thou wilt realize!*

When the door of thy friend's heart will be clos'd,

Thou shalt cry, as I cri'd until I becometh blind—
Clos'd is the door of thy friend,
Broken will be thine concourse of happiness!
Day's prolong'd hours thou shalt not withstand,
With struggle that burden of life thou wilt face,
That day thou wilt realize!

Bloom'd will be *dulon-chapa* again in the moon-lit spring night,
My bemoaning will resonate on the scatter'd stars of the sky quiet—
In the moon-lit spring night!
Seasons come time and again —
O my caress-phobic! In the blue sky thou wilt find
The star that look'd at thee the way I beheld
Thee with content and ease!
That day thou wilt realize!

A storm will come, the tempest will dance, all fetters will
Be shatter'd, in terror that day the hut will tremble;
Heart will cry for the broken ties! Thou shalt recall—
No more he is with thee, in the night the pain thou dost feel,
In thy cheek thou wilt want his kiss,
Beg him thou wilt for his touch, for his caress!
That day thou wilt realize!

The sore of my heart that would inflict thee with pain,
Being exhaust'd thou mayest hit me with that pain again —
The wayfarer will be there! Then on my lap thou wilt
Recline, may be willfully thou wilt put
Thy arms around me, my feet thou wilt kiss

And adore me—*that day thou wilt realize!*
(Dulonchapa)

A few words:
Poet knows she will recall him one day in many memories and realize how much he loved her. That day he will be no more with her.. in the torments of estrangement she will be lamenting.

The Call From The Back

O dear! when thou wilt be a part
Of a new household, wilt
Thou remember me then?
There will be thine new adoration
With new preparation!
That home where we met first--
Its shadow, its courtyard, its exuberance, its dust,
Its creepers and herbs--is now empty
And cries desolately!

O'er there when thou hadst forgotten me,
Came to meet thee
Many new faces, on my behalf in a fit of pique
That home would weep!
Where'er lookest thou, a pain of my
Memory thou feelest, in thy
New conversation this disgrace wilt thou forget,
Only me who was lost in
A forest of oblivion!

For so long a time that distance of mine was not real, O dear,
That old home made my distance much narrower!
Now thou hast new binding,
New accomplishment, new smiles, new crying,
Musical frenzy in new invocation!
In the old past lost was my melody of song!

O my friend! frustrat'd is my hope by being a boon of thy fate!

Today o'er my grave thy bridal-room will be built!
The melody of a bamboo flute I hear oll o'er the voidness,
In a pasture of wilderness~
At the setting-horizon I was lost!
Good bye, my friend, here is the end of game in this twilight
Hour of darkness! A new thou art
In the nook of a new abode!

A few words:
Poet's lover is now entangled with the life of a new person. Poet narrated here his memories with her lover that haunted him and called him from behind.

The Victorious

O my queen! At long last to thee I conced'd my defeat,
Tumbles down my flag of victory at thy feet,
My battle-conquering immortal sword makes me tir'd,
Day by day it becometh heavier,
Now conceding defeat I hand o'er that burden
To thee, my defeat-conceding-garland I entwine in thy bun!

O the goddess of life! Beholding me when didst thou drop tears?
Totter'd was that temple of the world-conqueror by thine tears.
Today O the victorious!
At the top of blood-stain'd chariot
Of the rebel the *anchal* of thine blue *sari* flutters throughout,
In thy garland today putting all my arrows I shed tears
Profusely, today I'm the conqueror!
[Chayanot]

A few words:
By being a king in his kingdom of love Poet conceded defeat to his queen, his lover. He made her victorious in the battle of his love. With all dignity and gracefulness of a king he made his submission wholly to the heart of his beloved. At the same time shedding tears of happiness with whole submission he declared himself a conqueror.

The Thorn of Lotus

Today, a jealousy I see there while in rut
With each other the elephants fight,
In my lotus garden only lotus thorns I behold,
With noises loud
To its brim the lake is fill'd and boisterous,
Asks off and on—'Who took away the blood-lotus
From my bosom? The swan will not dance
There listlessly with the swinging of waves!

When no lotus is there why those thorns prick me!
Today the curses of bathing-girl cast me down!
The maiden-wayfarer will come again?
Will she take my lotus-garland?
That pain of thorns only inflict my mind?
The lotus-thorns who'll tie in her
Bangle even though no lotus is there?
[Chayanot]

A few words:
Poet made the lotus as the symbol of love. But it is hard to win the heart of a lover. The pain of love is like the pain of thorns of lotus. He feels the pain of thorns but he sees no lotus.

The Poet's Queen

Thou lovest me, I'm a poet
Therefore! My whole being is the portrait
Of thy love manifested!
The sky, the breeze, the light of dawn,
The evening-star, the shining sun
Of the east- to me they extend'd
Hands as one of their own,--
Since thou dost love me,
They all loveth me!

In thy love the 'me' of mine was hidden,
All my hopes emerg'd at thy advent sudden!
'Tis thee who cometh to me
And in my sword thou playest the melody
Of flute, whate'er preparation to worship thee
I maketh is thine life's burnt-offerings, my words would be
Thy garland of victory, my queen!
To thee belongeth everything!

Thou lovest me, I'm a poet
Therefore! My whole being is the portrait
Of thy love manifested!
[Dolon-chapa]

A few words:
The Poet's Queen is his wife Pramila. The Poet dedicated his book of melody, 'Dolon chapa' to his beloved wife Pramila whom he called Dolon. He is a poet because she loves him. His whole being is a portrait of her love.

Paush (THE WINTER MONTH)

O the *Paush* has come!
The *Paush* has come
Traversing the sea of tears,
Sea of winter!
There she comes~ at the horizon she stands
In the veil of fog! She comes
And with pain of separation every leaf of trees cries,
Oh! Wife of *Ashta* looks with pensive sadness,
The navigating-lamp – the evening star
She lost there!

O the *Paush* has come~
With the exhaustion of travelling for one
Long year, with the abrasion
Of time, in the parting season of ripen
Paddy she is anxious
For coming new months,
O the *Paush* has come!
The *Paush* has come~
With dry breathing, with bemoaning
Wretch'd tone!
The voice I heard, 'Wake up, O the traveler!
Beyond a doleful look of my eyes you ought to go far!
[Dulon-chapa]

A few words:
Paush (The winter month) is like a lover who appeared after traversing many obstacles. She is anxious. She called the traveler, the poet, to wake up for a journey far away beyond the sight of her doleful eyes. She will never see him again..

Breeze Of Spring

Lost thou art in darkness—
Lost thou art ever since,
Today a mighty
Gap between thee and me!
Today is thine birthday~ at the time of remembrance
Sleepless I grope in the infinite darkness of oblivion!
Here in this place lost was my once recover'd garland!

Empty was the lake's deep dark water,
O the blue-lotus of pain! Why bloomest thou there?
The dark lake thou shinest,
Its tranquil waves thou breakest,~
Thy lotus was torn apart by which worshiper?
That lotus had cover'd which deity's stone-altar?

The boat of lost-jewels at the ferry of setting horizon
Cometh back every day from the village of rising horizon,
Oh! where is my jewel? Alone I'm in the *ghat*,
The swinging sea waves strike my chest!
In the crowd I look for a lotus-foot!

There blows again
The breeze of the spring,
In me I feel the grief,
Feel thy touch in errant breeze!
As usual the black bee-queen drinks
Mohua-nectar, intoxicat'd, she stoop'd down,
The *mohua*-forest swings,
Garden becometh restless
Amid flower-lavish'd southern breeze!

I recall -- *togor, chapa, bel, chamily, jui* bend
Down their branches when bees they behold!
Thou dost smile and swing the branches,
Red as rose thy chick flushes!
Tholkomli touches thy warm cheek! Seeing that *bokul*
Becometh anxious, land doth tremble!

Chirpings of nightingale become the *gazal* of spring night,
At noon the pigeons warbl'd in the courtyard!
The stars of the land—
Sajne shower'd petals on the swinging bun
Like Parch'd rice! The breeze blows there
Along with stoic voice of a kingfisher!

In deep *Piyal* forest embracing each other
The *Shaontal* girls drink glass-full of nectar,
From thy hideout thou didst watch
And say, 'I want such'!
A *chapa* I put in her bun, honey on her lips!
Sitting on a *Hizal* branch the cuckoo shrieks,
The *Dahuk* warbles and pegion dances in a still *lake*,
A join'd eye brow pattern the gulls make
And fly in the sky!
Suddenly thy feet touches the water nearby,
Shivers the black lake, blooms there red-lotus!
The blues of the lake would reflect in thy eyes!

Long time ago the noon is past, the day
Is about to go on the bank of the drowsy
Slumberous river! Conch blows in the tamples,
In the forest the darkness falls,

Oh! Darkness is carded in the branches of tamarisk,
Far away in the field a flute is blown from the stoic *polash* trees!

Dost thou put mango-bud-sticks in thy bun?
O dear! With coconut water dost thou clean
Thy face? Golden droppings from the wings of butterflies
Dost thou smear 'tween thy eyebrows?

Mangoes appear'd in clusters
When branch had no flowers,
The ripen'd *golapjam* are in pain,
Kamranga ripen'd again
To have the pain of mastication,
I remember,- thy cheek, thy bosom like a juicy *Jhamrul*!
No one doth evaluate that at all!

That furtive look from thy eyes
I would perceive,
A garland I would string
That I want,
Oh! No string I find! My mind-water is
Fill'd up with that look-like blue lotus!
Deep into my heart pierc'd the lotus-thorn!
There on my bosom tears dangle like strings of garland!
Where I shall anchor my boat! I find no shore,
The citrus flowers send the fragrance of memories
From afar! The blueish darkness crumples like poison
Over the *shal* forest! Like a Jewish-ear ring
Appears the moon in the darkness of evening!
O my trail, today I lost in a village unknown!

Where art thou!
Where am I now!
In the last
Spring we met,
In tearful eyes
This spring departs—

Thou art no more there!
Said a crying voice —where
Art thou settl'd now to live? Still thou stayest
Awake in the night
Longing for me? I look for the link that I lost
At the pallid hour of a day that I recover'd!

O dear! Here in a *ferry-ghat*
I anchor'd my boat!
With thy colorful feet
Thou mayest embark onto my boat,
Again with thy pleasing
Touch delightfully the boat will swing!
Together we shall go to a village by this boat,
There never shall we be lost,
O dear! Here in a *ferry-ghat*
I anchor'd my boat!
[Chayanot]

A few words:
When Poet's lover was no more with him he felt as if she was lost in darkness. She was like a blue lotus, bloomed gracefully in the dark-black water of lake. The poet was worried about the wellbeing of his blue lotus– some worshiper might have torn her apart and left her petals on the stone-altar! But in the tranquil breeze

of spring poet feels her presence in flowers, in fruits as he felt the same feelings in last the spring. He was longing for that moment when she would put her feet on the boat of his life he anchored in this ferry-ghat of world.

The Arrow-struck Bird

O the nestless arrow struck bird!
Your tender chest the arrow has pierc'd!
Where can I hide you and how?
Where's your wound, the pain you feel now?
Tears made me blind, nothing I can see,
O my jewel! To me 'tis not befitting to be
In pique now—the pain in you that I might arrest
Keeping you in my broken chest,
O my bird, your tender chest the arrow pierc'd thro'!
How and where can I hide you?

The arrow pierc'd the chest smear'd with poison!
Who holds you in the bosom, O the lost one?
Who show'd you the path towards my home?
Any relief you found in my home?
O my bird, your tender chest the arrow pierc'd thro'!
How and where can I hide you?

Ah! This place you look'd for comfort?
Here clouds rumble, wind rushes in gust,
Trembles the little hut!
In fierce storm my lamp is blown out, all doors are broken,
The endless weeping of bereft nights off and on
Dangles in my heart!
O my bird,
Your tender chest the arrow pierc'd thro'!
In such a foul day where can I hide you?

The dear son welcomes death, stands at the door
Of this powerless mother,

The jewel I recover'd, lost it again and again,
Oh! In fear my heart trembles lest you leave me again!
O my lost-jewel, O my bird! How
And where can I hide you?

O my lost jewel that
I once recover'd,
To me you're known instantly,
O come unto me, for a moment let me
Hold you, seeing your wound when
No one picks you up, can
A mother perpetual abandon you? Scar'd
Of losing you she is not!
O my bird, your tender chest the arrow pierc'd thro'!
How and where can I hide you?

'Tis the ever-known affection, my guest you're not,
Nor relat'd to me in the past,
With new identity time and again you came
In this home!
O dear, stay as many days you want to stay
In mother's bossom! Can the mother of the day
Of creation keep you away!
To be getting lost? Perhaps
A deception to eyes!
[Chayanot]

A few words:
This poem is about the grief-stricken helpless poet like a nestless arrow struck bird whose heart was overcast with distress and dismay. But a graceful woman provided him with shelter and love with motherly affection though she was not blood related to him.

The Fleeing Water Bird

O *choka*, from afar what melodic note
Of a flute thou hast heard?
O my fleeing bird of water!
Which lost home thou couldst remember?
Which land of riches in thy dream appears?
O my fleeing bird of water!
With tears in thy lively eyes tell me~
Thy mother called thee?
Standing at the horizon under the shadow
Of clouds she beckon'd thee in deep love!
O the anxious derang'd! Thou knowest her?
As if with deep affection she calleth~, 'Come, O dear,
Come unto my lap, come unto me closer,
O my naughty baby! O my fleeing bird of water!'

Southern breeze has shudder'd the forest,
O my darling child!
At last thou hast
Known—who's thy kindred and who's not!
The darkness cover'd my home in early dawn,
On the paddy ears, in the whistling of green
Crops- O sweet baby! Tell me, what made thee startl'd suddenly,
The bond of love thou hast broken instantly!
Tears melt down in thy eyes! Someone gave thee poison—
The drink of affection!
Call'd a baby-rabbit all on a sudden
'Come O baby, the loving one
To the wilderness, come back, O the fleeing bird
Restless!' O the *Choka* of the wild!

A few words:

In this poem the Poet perceived the feeling of a lost, lonely, young water bird away in wilderness from her mother bird. Poet feels the agonies of the panicked baby bird as if Poet was that baby who lost his mother for a while in the wilderness!

[Chayanot]

The Eternal Baby

O thou nameless infant-traveler, traversing an unknown land
Thou hast arriv'd! Which bangle has adorn'd thy hand
Today, what kind of confinement
Is this for the unbridl'd one? Tell me,
In which name shall I call thee
Again with my content'd heart?
A lost wayfarer thou art,
In this house thou hadst lived, O thou hadst
Come time and again when thy identity was lost!

O dear, O my jewel, the jewel in a dark house!
With little bit of cream thou hast fill'd this
Hungry home with thy little hand, in profound happiness
Today an ocean of tears heaves
In my heart; while calling thee
With new name, Oh! Who stops me!
Why my heart's getting heavy!
Traveler, thou hast come from a setting horizon
While wending thy way towards the rising dawn!
[Chayanot]

A few words:
The poet is an eternal-baby. His lover knows no confinement can hold him in. She loves this wayfarer-poet. She calls him with contented heart by the name she wants to call. The eternal baby came from the setting horizon and departed again towards the rising dawn.

At The Time Of Farewell

O dear! Look not at me time and again with tearful eyes,
O look not at me with tearful eyes!
Sing no farewell song with bereav'd broken
Tone, sing no farewell song!

Lifelong pain thou hast suppress'd
With smile, then smile today too, shed no tears at
Parting time, that painful eyes, that face about to weep I see,
In torment my heart roars in me!
Traveler! O the traveler of far distance – Oh! Such
A way cover not thy travelling path with pitiless
Songs and tears!

O dear! Cover not thyself with tears!
O the distant traveler! Thou thinkest no one
Understands thy pain! Thou only feelest thy pain!
On the roads wander the wayfarers,
No home-dwellers
Finds them out, pain in heart appears still as a sore?
Baul song drifts across the barren fields from afar!
That fills the traveler's heart with grief?
'Tis thy wrong fit of pique! O stranger of a foreign land!
The loss thou dost care the home dwellers had incurr'd!
But knowest thou!
For thee many broken hearts now
Weep secretly in parting time somewhere!
O traveler! O dear resentful distant traveler!
Go not with pain—
Thinking that no one

Had lov'd thee, O dear, if thou dost want to go, go then,
But go not with pain!
[Chayanot]

A few words:
In the journey of life the poet was a distant-traveler to travel far away. He was at the departing time of his life to leave his beloved and many others behind who loved him so much. His sweet beloved urged him not to depart from them with tears in eyes, with pain in heart but with smiles.

A Distant Friend

From which far-off lonely village O my friend
Thou dost call me in a painful tone?
Oftentimes gusty wind
Shatters my wayside home of pain,
Homeless I'm, I roam around!

Thy flute's stoical crying slackens all fetters!
To adore a wayfarer is my job—and to find out there
A road-friend while wandering around—
Away, far away! O my belov'd!
For so little a thing
Envious thou becomest, so on my path I take no sojourn —
In my heart I feeleth thy pain!

Tearful are thine eyes, a home thou wantest to build
By roadside, blows the northern wind
O'er the wet grass, the deep sighs are heav'd and
Tears are shed with thy melodies, O my friend !
[Chayanot]

A few words:
He is a friend of far-off village who roams around here and there. Though the poet lives far away but his heart is tied with her heart.

His melody of pain calls her from a land afar. The memory of his love like the tone of his flute slackens all bindings of life. She heaves a sigh, her tears are shed like melancholic melody of the flute that drifts along.

The Evening Star

O dear evening star, whose veil'd-bride art
Thou? Which lost face dost
Thou perceive in thine eyes? With thy *anchal* thou coverest
The evening lamp, thy glimpse shivers
As thou lookest sidelong at thine lover's
Arrival path in every dark evening, here
In the same manner!

Unto a bereav'd heart of a homeless
A lost-bride thou walkest silently in the darkness
Of the setting sun! This coming and going
In recurrent manner, this pathetic gloomy looking,
For whom all these, O the sky-bride!
Today someone dear thou hast lost!
[Chayanot]

A few words:
The evening star is a gloomy veiled girl to poet; like a lost bride she walks along in the darkness of the setting day. The poet deemed the evening star as a melancholic new bride who might have lost someone dear today!

The Pain Of The Deep Night

In this quiet deep night only tears
Come into my eyes! What are those words
Of thine I recall! Why are they so radiant?
In my bosom whose apathy doth resonate?
In my heart growls which cry in utter
Frustration and filleth my eyes with tears!

My pain of futile life in this deep night
I could not hide,
Alone in my sleep only tears dropeth quietly,
That night was also a night lonely,
When desires uncountable arous'd in my heart,
The forlorn breath of those desires is blend'd
With pain of morning *purobi* raga
And flaccid *shefalika!*
[Chayanot]

A few words:
The pain of frustration and resentment brought many questions to poet's mind in deep night. In futile he tried to hide his pain and many desires that aroused in his heart blended with morning purobi raga and flaccid jasmine.

Hope

May be
There I'll find thee,
Where sky bends down and kisses
The forest's green edges!
In a far-off village field,
Or on a little ridge of crop field,
Or in a lonely *ghat*
Perhaps alone thou wilt come and with
A smile my hand thou wilt grip!

Thy unveiled glances at the edge
Of that impenetrable blue, that northern breeze-
The horizon's secret emissary brought
Thy arrival tidings! O dear, naughty thou art,
Through the gaps of forest
Thou wilt come, and kiss
Tenderly on my eyes,
Those memories are written
There in the crimson hue of horizon!
[Chayanot]

A few words:
Poet hopes that he will find his beloved in his imaginary places- in the blue edge of horizon, or near a green forest or on the ridge of crop field or in a lonely ghat when a northern breeze sways along. All those memories are written in the crimson hue of horizon.

Thirsty For One's Own Self

The one—so dearest to me, more than
My own being,
In my own self I look for her!
As if the sound of her footsteps I hear
In my own thirsty desire!

In my mind's thirsty sky screams that
Crest'd cuckoo with ardent thirst,
Sometime as a *chukor* she comes,
Ambrosia she steals
In the dream of night,
In a moon-lit night!

In my mind's *Piyal* and *Tomal* woods
I behold her in greens and clouds,
In the light of thunderbolts,
In one bright pleasing
Pause of lightning!

Sitting in my own garden I adorn'd
Her with a garland I craft'd!
I woke up, Oh! All on a sudden I found
Around my neck dangles that garland!
[Chayanot]

A few words:
When the love for the beloved is merged with one's own-self then he can behold his love exists everywhere,... whatever things he sees around him he finds his beloved there.

Today Frenzi'd Is My Mind-Bee

In the field of pea-pod, in the flowers of grass,
O dear, today frenzi'd is
My mind-bee!

In this morn of sun-caress'd winter
With a restless butterfly from flower to flower
I fly around, slurping flowery nectar!
In the fields, in the streams I hear
The wailing of parting paddy of winter!

Who breathes there on cat-kins near
The bank of dead river !
She walks, Oh! With the flowers of pea-pods her
Yellow *anchal* entwines, her nose-ring—the *babla* flower,
Sari is her blue *oparajita*, I go for
A stolid touch of that unknown girl there.
While walking on a path nearby field
With her eyes me she beckon'd!

In the field of pea-pod, in the flowers of grass,
O dear, today frenzi'd is
My mind-bee!
(Chayanot)

A few words:

On a bright day of the sun-caress'd winter the joyous poet found himself near a field of pea-pod. His mind flies like a bee, like restless butterfly it moves from flowers to flowers. He wants to feel the stolid touch of a wanton village belle who cast a glance at him while walking on a path nearby the field.

Beware, O The Helmsman!

Chorus:
Mountain, wilderness, desert, and the sea endless
In the deep dark night thou hast to traverse,
Beware, O the travelers!

In the swelling waves the boat swings,
Boatman loses the navigation, torn is
The sail, the helm who will hold?
Who has that courage? Any stout
Young man out there!
Come forward, calleth thee the future!
In this storm terrible the sea thou hast to cross,
Boat is to be taken onto the shore!

O the sentries of the mother land, beware!
Dark is the night everywhere!
The heap'd up pain through ages hath declar'd
This expedition! In depriv'd bosom foams up the amass'd
Resentment, on the way thou shalt have to pick them up,
The rights they have!

There drowns the helpless nation,
It knows not how to swim! O the helmsman!
Thee we shall watch today what oath hast thou taken
To liberate thy mother land!
'Are they Hindus or Muslims?' Who asketh that? Helmsman!
Say, 'Drowning in the water are the human beings,
They're my mother's progenies!'

Mountainous gorge, rumbling thunder, frighten'd

Are the travelers, suspicious are those who lagg'd behind!
Helmsman! Art thou in difficult navigation?
Wantest thou to give up in mid-ocean?
With each other they fight and whine,
This burden thou art to pull on as the onus is thine!

Helmsman! Behold there the field of *Polashi*,
Where *Clive's* sword was stain'd with blood of *Bangali*!
Oh! In the Ganges the sun of India is drown'd!
With shining blush our blood-smear'd sun will rise again!

On the gallows those who sang the song of triumph of life
Stood silently, unnotic'd— ready to sacrifice!
An ordeal today— whom they'll salvage,
Nation or the caste? The boat swings
In the swelling waves, beware, O the helmsman!
[Shorbohara]

A few words:
In this awakening chorus song the poet depicted the entire India as a storm-stricken boat in the middle of an enraged sea. The Poet is encouraging the helmsman and giving him hope that the sun of India will rise again that was drowned in the river Ganges. The Poet asked the helmsman to take control of the sinking boat. In the stormy dark night the expedition was carried out by the struggling people of India who were savagely suppressed and oppressed by the ruler.

Song Of The Students

We're the force, we're the strength,
We're the student party,
At our feet the storm swoons,
Up above— the sky and wind,
We're the student party!

Journey we make on the stumbling road
On bare feet in dark night,
Our bloody feet stain'd the ground
While we walk'd with steps strong!
Through ages our blood drench'd the earth,
We're the student party!

Our aimless life is like a comet out of its orbit!
At her slaughtering altar victims we become
In the hand of the goddess of destiny!
When *Laksmi* ascends the heaven,
Into the bottomless blue we descend!
We're the student party!

We hold the rein of sacrificial horse of the king of death,
The history of our life our death writes!
In the land of laughter we bring devastating tears!
We're the student party!

Mistakes we make when everybody works with skills!
Careful people build dams, the shore we break then!
Our blood makes the road slippery in the night terrible,
We, the young! We're the student party!

In our eyes illuminates the torch of wisdom ~
Chest full of words,
We voice—the unhesitating call of eternity!
Our fresh blood makes the white lotus red!
We're the student party!

On that devastating flood we sacrific'd our lives,
Within us moans the freedom of twentieth century!
Mother's blue *anchal* we fill with red tears!
We're the student party!

We build the future of love, future of hope,
Milkyway shows us light towards heaven's path,
In our eyes let the dream of
The people of the world come true!
We're the student party!
[Sarbohara]

A few words:
Poet wrote many awakening songs for the youths. It is one of them. He perceived the younger generation as courageous and invigorated who are ready to sacrifice. They can illuminate the torch of freedom for their motherland with hard works and strong determination.

My All-enduring Mother

All-enduring
O my mother, all-sacrificing
Thou art! On trial thou didst put none
Nor didst thou accuse anyone!
Cries alone a reticent daughter at the shore of pain
Like a lost timid village girl unknown,
Thyself thou dost ask 'Where am I now?'
From afar the stars call thee, 'come, come hither!'
Absconding daughter thou art arriv'd here
By mistake tracing the milky-way! Law
And lawlessness have beaten you,
O My mother! Oh! exists in thine eyes still a painful query –
The reason for persecution! Who are they?
All those sorrows, pain and grief, whatever it be?
Still unknown are the reasons to thee,
O the daughter of *Oloka!* So speechlessly, silently thou didst
Endure! Fire burns the incense, the incense knows not!
Here comes boys and girls from far off place,
For a mnoment they pause as they look at thy face!
Thee they ask, 'Wilt thou be our mother?'
Thou dost embrace them mulling over
For a moment, in motherly affection
Eyes are tearful, know thou dost everyone,
Thou art known!
To thy home they come like children
Of a foreign land!
Saying two words to thee:'My mother',
With a hug they leave thee there!
One day in a tiredsome voice ask'd thee a desert bedouin

Boy-'Thou wilt be my mother?' he return'd not again,
He left, to this day memory of his graveyard
Pricks thy heart feebly, or no more exists he in thy heart!
Mind can bear so many memories,
Many memories it loses...

O my mother all-enduring! Never
Remains empty a heart of a mother and the creator!
In thy heart those who fumble –perhaps
In their memories this depriv'd boy still exists!
[Sarbohara]

A few words:
Poet wrote the above poem on Birojasundari Devi, depicting her as an all-enduring mother. In 1920s poet had a chance to know two elderly ladies. He found tremendous affection and love from these two elderly ladies- they were Birojasundari Devi, whom he called 'Ma' (mother) and her sister-in-law, Giribala Devi, whom he called 'Mashima'(aunty). Pramila, the wife of the poet, was the teen-aged daughter of Giribala Devi. They lived in a town named Comilla which is now in Bangladesh.

A Struggling Poor Man

Surround'd by deep water of pain
In a little quicksand island
A home you built there?
What a mad you're!
In the sky the lightning shimmers,
Awful din he made the struggling poor man!
O'er his head like tears rain pours down,
From afar the land beckons
Him with swinging trees!

There your worried daughters are weeping,
Affectionately the sea is calling
Them, sail your boat today, O boatman!
In the waves the storm swings like a horse, O boatman!
How long will you wait? Pull off the anchor of illusion!

On your shatter'd courtyard the day-light
Is getting dim! Boatman! Casts she glance your sweet heart
From the river bank! There goes her companion!
Getting deeper the night of monsoon,
Oh! Sleep not on a mat full of weeping!
Is it your liability to break the bond of crying?

You want'd not diamond and jewels,
You need no money in millions,
Only a small earthen-pot you need'd — fill'd up with indigence!
A torn-mat-full of sleep weariless
You want'd—a hut illuminat'd by a lamp feebly!
Comes there death, a burglar and senility.

O boatman, drift your boat o'er the land!
Let your feet be stain'd with blood
With every stroke on the land hard!
O the cataclysmic traveler, on
Your way you trample hills, forest and mountain!
Downpour heralds the monsoon,
The sea dances around!
O the traveler of water, now move forward
O'er the land!
[Sharbohara]

A few words:
Poet conceived this little quicksand island as troubled life of struggling people with pain and miseries.

The life of poor struggling people is always filled with indigence. They need no money in millions, but a weariless sleep and a little lamp to light their home. The poet is urging the poor struggling boatman that time has come to drift his boat over the land.

The Song Of Equality I Sing

The song of equality I sing —
Where all obstacles and differences are merg'd into one,
Where blend'd together are all Hindus-Buddhists-Muslims and
Christians! The song of equality I sing!
Who art thou? A Persian? Jaina? Jew? Or *Shaotal, Veel, Garo*?
Confucius? Follower of Charvac? Go on, tell me more!
My friend, whoe'er thou art, whate'er
Books and scriptures
Dost thou carry on
Thy belly, back, shoulder or in brain,
Quran-Puran-*Veda-Vedanta*-Bible-Tripitak, Zend-Avesta,
Granth Sahib! Read as many as thou cravest
For— but why all this futile effort!
Why art thou so desperate?
Why this bargaining in the flowers' shop—
When fresh flowers on the roadside doth bloom?
Within thee lie the wisdom of all ages and scriptures,
O my friend, open thy heart, all scriptures are there!
Incarnations of all ages, all religions inhere in thy soul,
Thy heart, the world-temple is for the God of all,
In dead scriptures and skeletons lookest thou for God?
From the concealment of thy seclud'd heart God
Smileth! I tell not a lie, my friends,
To this heart boweth down all the royal crowns!
This heart is the *Nilachal, Kashi, Mathura, Brindaban*,
'Tis Buddha-Gaya, Jerusalem, Medina,
Mosque, Temple, church and Ka'aba!

Whilst sitting here the truth Jesus and Moses found!

In this battle field the young flute-boy sang
The great *Geeta*, in this pasture the shepherd-prophets
Became the friends of God! Whilst sitting in this cave of heart,
Shakyamuni abandon'd the kingdom as he perceiv'd
Unbearable pain of mankind, in this cave the Arab-belov'd
Heard the call of the Almighty!
From here sang he the message of equality
Of the Qur'an!
O my friends,
Nothing untrue I heard,
No temple or Ka'aba is greater than this heart!
[Shamyabadi]

A few words:

The philosophy of the universal equality of mankind is the central theme of the poem. All differences and hindrances that exist in the religion and society of mankind need to be merged at one confluence of equality. When the entire mankind will take the message of equality in their hearts, the injustice and oppression will cease immediately. As he wrote, wisdom of equality lies in the heart, not in the scriptures of religions.

The Creator

O brother, who art thou looking for the Lord
All over the earth and heavens! Dost
Thou wander in the wilderness,
On the peak of mountains?
Oh! The sages and saints,
Holding the precious jewel on
Bosom, stride ye from land to land
In search of the Lord!
The creation looks unto thee but thine eyes are clos'd,
Look unto the Creator—but with thyself busy thou art!

Wishful-blind! Open thine eyes,
In the mirror lookest thou at thine image,
Wherein God thou wilt see!
Make not him a hero, fear not him as he
Is vers'd in scripture! 'Private Secretary' of God he is not!
God is amidst all, the Omnipotent !
The unseen Creator I discern whence I look at me!
With jewels the merchants trade on the shore of sea,
By mistake inform them not about the quarry of gems!
Quarry they know think the traders
When jewels they see!
At the bottom of the deep sea
They div'd not, friends, dive
Into the sea of truth, ignore the scriptures ye keep!
[Shamyabadi]

A few words:
In poet's view God's image is concealed within our own soul and body.

It is not mandatory to look for the Creator in the place of seclusion, here and there. He urged us to look for the truth, the Creator, in our own self instead of spending time in search of scriptures.

The Mankind

The song of equality I sing—
Nothing's nobler and greater than mankind;
Exists there no difference in place, time and person;
Indistinguishable are the religion and nation;
He is the kinsman of mankind of all places,
Of all times, in every house!—
'O priest, open the door! The god of hunger
Knocks thy door,
'Tis the time to worship!' Having a dream the anxious priest
Open'd the temple door and thought
Today perchance a king he would
Be by the boon of god!
But clad in torn-rag a sickly
Wayfarer said feebly:
'Open the door, please! I haven't eaten for days'!
Abruptly the priest shut the temple door on his face,
'Twas a dark night; hungry wayfarer turn'd
Back, his hunger-jewel shin'd his path all around!
The man whin'd aloud,
'Temple belongeth not to thee, but to the priest, O God.'
Yesterday in the mosque an oblation was offer'd,
Left over meat and bread made the *molla* delight'd!
There a wayfarer with distress all over his body appear'd,
Said, 'O father, I'm hungry, for seven days without food!'
In annoyance niggardly *molla* whimper'd, 'A trouble maker
Indeed! 'Hungry thou art! Land fill'd with dead cows, go over there!
Dost thou pray, plebeian?' The hungry repli'd,
'No, father, I pray not.' The *molla* yell'd,

'Then get lost, thou scamp!' Holding bread and meat
He lock'd the mosque-door and left!
The hungry wayfarer walk'd away, mutter'd a complaint—
'Eighty years I pass'd, my Lord, thee I never call'd!
Never didst thou stop my food totally! Lord!
The rights on thy temple and mosque people had lost!
All doors are lock'd by those *mollas* and priests!'
Where is *Gazni Mahmud, Kalapahar,* Genghis?
Break those lock'd-doors of the house of worship!
Who bolts the doors, puts them under lock and
key? Doors should be kept open ever!
Break the bolt with hammer and crowbar!
Oh! The house of worship! From thy minaret
Sing the hypocrites the song of selfinterest!
Hating mankind who kisses desparately
On Qur'an, Veda and Bible! Snatch the holy
Books away from their mouths, slaying mankind
The books they brought,
Hypocrites worship the scriptures! Listen! All the ignorants,
Men brought the scriptures, scriptures brought no man!
Adam, Abraham, Moses, Jessus, David,
Krishna, Buddha, Nanak, Muhammad,
Kabir happen'd to be the treasures of the universe,
Our fathers and fore-fathers,
Their blood we carry more or less
In our veins and arteries!
By being their sons, kith and kin we resemble them,
Who knows, great men like them one day we might become!
Friend, laugh not! How unfathomable deep is 'me' of mine,
I know not for sure, may live in me glorifi'd someone!

Perchance in me lives the last incarnation of *Vishnu*; in thee,
The Jesus, the *Mehdi* !
Who knows whose ending and beginning, who finds whose trace?
O brother, whom dost thou kick? Whom dost thou hate?
May be in his heart liveth the God day and night!
Or may be he's nothing of that sort, nor that high and great,
With sores and wounds liveth he within the whirl-pool
Of sorrows, no holy books, no places holier than that of the ignoble!
A child he might beget in this thatch'd hut, an ever
Matchless man he could be! The man with great power,
His message not heard of, not even seen by the world,—
Perhaps 'tis he who was born in that thatch'd hut!

A *Chandal* startles thee? He ain't a despicable animal !
Harischandra or *Shiva* of crematorium he could be! Today's *chandal*,
Tomorrow a great sage-emperor he might become!
His invocation thou wilt recite, thou wilt adore him!
Him thou dost neglect as a shepherd?
Perhaps covertly *Gopal* of *Braja* appear'd
In disguise of a shepherd,
As rustic ploughman him thou loathest!
Perhaps *Balaram* disguis'd
Himself as a ploughman! All shepherd-prophets
Took the control of helm, one eternal
Message they brought – 'tis still a message and perpetual
It will remain! Being rebuk'd the beggar-man and maid walk'd away!

In them lies the *Bholanath* and *Girijaya*, do I recognize any
   way!
Lest alms giving make thy food short thou hast beaten
Her with door-stick and driven
The goddess away! Record'd was that act
Of cruelty –who knows the disgrac'd goddess forgave thee
   or not!

Friend! Greedy thou art, thy eyes are cover'd with flaps of
   selfishness!
Or else thou couldst have seen a goddess
Serv'd thee by being a servant!
In the heart left whate'er godliness, pain-churn'd
Ambrosia, dost thou want to plunder?
Wantest thou to appease thine greedy hunger?
In hunger what food
Thou didst eat
Thine disorder'd stomach only knows !
In which part of thine palace the death-arrow lies?
Thine lascivious queen! In every bygone epoch the animal
Within thyself pull'd thee down into the death hole!
[Shamyabadi]

A few words:
Poet asserted that the humanity is the virtue of mankind. Humanity stands above all caste, race and religion. Greedy and selfish people use the religion and race as their own weapon to fulfill their lust. Many great men in this world came out from ordinary background. No one knew a child could be a great man in future. Again mankind is prone to greed and lust. Men can succumb to lust, charm and deceit.

Sin

The song of equality I sing! The penitents and sinners—
They're all my sisters, my brothers,
In this sin-world any man or woman there commit'd no sin?
Never mind us;--the sinners' helmsman is mir'd with sin!
With the sin of million gods that heaven trembles,
Through the gods' passage of sin enter the devils
Into heaven, from Adam till Nazrul
More or less everyone by the knife of vice
Slaughter'd the virtue! Abode of vice is this
World! With God its half is fill'd,
Half with devil!
All fanatics! Listen,
Before counting other's sin, count thy own sin!
In the mud of vice grows virtuous lotus,
In every flower the sin sprouts!
Curse and deceptions is all over this beauteous
Earth, in the past succumbed to obnoxious
Traps a good many incarnations, the soul and life
They submitt'd to virtue, body to vice.
The truth I told, my friend,
Brahma, Vishnu, Shiva, never mind
The ordinary people; the hermits, the saints,
Meditators and yogis –
Their souls were ascetic and dedicat'd,
But to earthly pleasure their body tend'd!
Abode of vice is this world! Here mounts the empty sac
Of virtue on the back
Of religion-donkey, here all are equal sinners,
By our own weights of sin we weigh the sin of others!

Why so much grandeur of accountability if thou wert
A godly person? Putting a cap on head
Or a *tiki* at the back of head thou dost pretend to be a sinless!
Why this ostentatious show, so much wantonness
Of trademarks? As if wearing police uniform escap'd
A criminal convict'd!

Friend, a story I'll tell thee interesting,
Once all sinless angels gather'd in heaven blaming
The norms of the destiny, they said,
So much we worship god,
Glorify Him day and night, still not happy He is, all affection,
Mercy He bestows on
The sin inflict'd clay-made mankind! God heard it,
Told them in smiling,—'They're the progeny of dust,
Ordinary, weak mind'd.' Exists there
The pain of mistakes in every flower,
Curse in every lips and eyes, desires in *chandan*,
Warmth of kiss in moon!
Charming women are there with collyrium in eyes,
Ornament'd lace around their waste,
Feet colour'd with shellac, *tambul* in mouth, seeing all these
The god of love is dumbfounded! With their greedy eyes
The Satans stare! On their back they carry flower-bows,
In the eyes the flower-arrows!
Said the angels, 'Lord, we want to see there how the earth
Works, how flowers bloom with the imminence of senility and death!'
Said the God, 'Let the best two amongst ye enter
Into earth and see the awful enticement there.'
Haruth, Maruth, the pride of the angels have enter'd

Into earth, they're the part
Of the sun, moon and the earth's dust,
They stepp'd into the dwellings of mankind, wherein lies illusion
Of every form, traps with every shadow, there the moon
Reflects in lotus-lake! Here color, sound and smell
Are the gallow's trap, pitcher-full of smiles
Reverberate on every pond's bank, from the field
The melody of flute emanates! Doused are the impassion'd
Angels with earthly essence, their hearts are scratch'd
By the gaze captivating women beautiful!
With the sound of shining cymbals
There goes the concubine *zohora* spilling water
From the pitcher! Overwhelm'd with her
Beauty the angels tumbl'd to her opalescent feet,
Into pomegranate juice their lips are dipp'd,
No more fear they had for the hell fire,
Got rowdy whilst drinking grape wine from earthen *sorai* !
Self-control they lost!
Breaking barriers of prohibition with content
They drank wine from the earthen pot,
Wine spill'd all over lips, flowers and bangles!
In smiling God spoke to heaven's angels,
'Behold! *Haruth* and *Maruth* spoil'd the earth, a massacre indeed!'
Confidante, in this earth the eyes know the magic!

Thousand years' devotion may vanish by one wink of eye,
O the charming earth, the ever youthful! Thy
God is not *Shiva* - but *kama* and *roti*!
[Shamyabadi]

A few words:

In this poem the poet emphasized on the fact that none of us is perfect; we all commit sin on occasion. Everyone of us more or less slaughtered the virtue by the knife of vice. The world is an abode of vice and deception. He pleaded us to count our own sin first before we count others. The fruit of spiritual bliss one earned through many days' devotion may vanish in one wink of eye if he slips from the right path by committing a sin.

The Whore

O mother,
Who calleth thee a whore,
Who doth spit at thee?
A mother as chaste as *Shita* might have suckl'd thee!
Though not a chaste,
The same lineage
Thou canst claim to our mothers and sisters,
Thy sons are like ours,
Our kith and kin; like us the fame
They deserve, respect, reputation and name,
With devotion strenuous they can
Reach the door of heaven,
Drona the son of celestial whore *Gritachi*; the great
Warrior, a virgin's son, *Krishna Dvaipayana*, a rever'd;
Karna, a son born to a virgin mother,
A great charity donor and a warrior!
From heaven came down *Ganga*, found *shiva* her husband,
To *Ganga* king *Shantonu* offer'd his love again,
Their sons, *Bhisma and Krishna*; the Book tells—a truthful sage
Was a speaking-baby of virgin mother! A strange
Birth he had, the great Jesus! Nobody is sinner
And filthy, no body hateful here!
In the wish-lake of *Kalidaha* there bloom'd
Millions of lotus unblemish'd!
Listen to mankind's message,
Just after birth human being carries no remorse!
No right I've on virtue since sin I committ'd?
For their sins uncountable Gods' godliness is not fad'd,

If *Ahallya* could achieve liberation, mother Mary be the holiest,
Why wilt thou not be rever'd as pure and chaste?
Scorns thee which fanatic for having an illegitimate child?
O God I ask thee— a billion and half children liveth in this world,
How many parents wish'd to have a son and daughter in platonic love?
How many parents were ingenuous and chaste?
How many of them meditat'd to have a child in earth?
How many million suckling babies died at birth?
Simply with animal passion men and women meet here,
We, the children are the outcome of that greedy desire!
Yet, a great pride doth we bear!
Listen,O the religious mentors—
I perceive not any difference between a child
Misbegotten and a child born in lust!
If a son of an unchaste mother is illegitimate,
Then a child born to an amoral father is bastard indeed!
[Shamyabadi]

A few words:

In this poem the poet addressed a prostitute as his mother. He perceived that prostitute is not sinful since she was breast-fed by a noble chaste mother in her infancy. The society and poverty led her to the path of prostitution. He perceived that there was no difference between a child misbegotten and a child born in lust. He asserted, if a child of a mother is born without wedlock becomes illegitimate, then a child born to an amoral father is bastard indeed.

The Woman

The song of equality I sing —
See I not any difference between a man and woman!
All deeds great and e'er-beneficial were done
In this world, half of them was accomplish'd by woman,
The rest half by the man.
Equally in this world men and women
Brought all sins, sufferings, tears and pain.
O woman, who doth loathe thee as a pit infernal?
Tell him, the sinner primordial
Was not the woman, 'twas the satan!
Or whoe'er a sinner or a satan—
'Tis neither a man nor a woman, a neuter 'tis!
Equally in man and woman it exists!
To all flowers and fruits women gave beauty, taste,
Sweetness and flavor, seest thou not
The stone of *Tajmohal*? Its life there?
In its inner core lies *Momotaj*, *Shahjahan* in its outer!
Woman, the *Lakshmi* of knowledge, music and crops,
'Tis the graceful woman who changes into many forms!
The scalding heat of sun of a day a man brings,
Woman brings peace of night, breeze and clouds!
Courage and strength they impart
During the day, wives they become at night,
With desert-thirst man appears,
While charm and sweetness woman offers.
Crop-fields get fertil'd as man ploughs,
Planting crops woman brings lustrous
Green, man tills, woman waters the soil, together water
And soil bring forth crops that dazzle in the golden paddy
    ears!

A mass of silver or gold becometh ornaments
Whene'er it adorns the body of a woman.
The man was induc'd with poetic spirit in his separation
And union with woman,
Whate'er he spoke 'twas a poem, whate'er he sound'd
'Twas a music! In course of time a great child
Of a great man was born when man with desire,
Woman with passion met together.
All victories, adventures in this world were glorifi'd
As mothers, sisters and wives made
Their sacrifice, history wrote many men in the battle had
Shed blood, but not about many women who were widow'd!
Kind-heart'd mothers, sisters render'd their service,
Their names are not found on the memorial stone of the heroes?
Victorious was not the men's sword alone, women inspir'd them,
Energiz'd them! The King governs his kingdom,
Queen governs her king, queen's sympathy
Took away all kingdom's ignominy!
Heartless are the men!
To make them human all women
Offer'd them half of their hearts! Immortal
Great men with fame monumental
Ceremonially every year them we remember,
Just out of whim their foppish fathers
Have begotten them! In the forest
Rama left *Lova* and *kusha*; *Shita* brought
Them up! The woman taught a baby affection,
Love, kindness, and compassion,
But decorat'd her own bright eyes with collyrium of pain!

In a queer way, the haughty, rude man paid up
That debt, the child she kiss'd with affection and love,
Put her in the prison!
He was the man-incarnation—
Slew his mother with an axe as his father commanded!
Half of the world's women now ignore men's demand —
For many years women were suppress'd, now subdu'd are the men!
Those days are bygone!

Slaves in the past were not the men but the women!
Now 'tis the era of humanity, equality and pain,
Nobody's captive to nobody; the beating of drums all around!
In prison men put the women,
After many years
The sufferings and death they face
In the same prison made for women!
'Tis the norm of the time— if thou dost torment someone,
Inflicts thee back that pain of torment indeed.
Listen, O creatures of the world!
More dost thou oppress someone,
Thou becomest more unmanly! Tell us, O the woman,
Who was that tyrant made thee prisoner
In *Yaksa's* city fill'd with treasure?
All that zeal thou hast lost today, scar'd thou art!
From behind the scenes thou speakest!
Thou canst not put eyes on eyes; bangles
Are on thine wrists, bangles 'round the ankles,
O women, take the timid veil off! Break the fetter!
Remove that spot of slavery, embellishment whatsoe'er!
O the loving daughter of the earth! No more thou dost

Wander in the mountains, caves and woods
While singing with birds!
When the death king Pluto arriv'd on his wings at night?
He snatch'd and put thee in his dark house!
'Tis thy primitive bondage!
Dead thou art in the city of death;
That day the night shroud'd the earth;
Destroy that city O mother! Get up like a *Nagini*
From the bottom of earth! Broken bangles will guide thee
In the darkness, the dog of hunger is releas'd
And tumbl'd down! Long since thou hast
Been offering them ambrosia, now 'tis a necessity,
Offer them intricate poison!
Not far away that day—when the world will sing the song
Of triumph of women along with men!
[Shamyabadi]

A few words:
In his poem Poet expressed strongly his view on women's equality in the society and their importance in the society along with men. He stated in his poem that women's contributions in the society are enormous since time immemorial. They should not be slaved, tortured and neglected by the man.

Cooli

In a train that day
A foppish man push'd a guy
Out of the bogie,
For he was a *cooli*!
Deeply it offend'd me!
Weaker people all o'er the world be treat'd
Like this? The train wherein the foppish board'd
And knock'd down a cooli is
Fuel'd and run by the bones of *dodichi*!

Shut up all the liars! You paid up their wages? You earn'd
How much million rupee paying
Them how much *pai*? Ships in the sea, automobiles
On the highways, trains on the railroads,
Machines all o'er- who brought all these?
Tell me, whose blood is anoint'd on those buildings you own? ~
Remove spectacles from your eyes, see written
There all answers on the bricks!
You know not, but dust in streets
Know those ships, railways and buildings!
Ahead are good days, increas'd are their liabilities
Eventually, debt they ought to pay,~ with the hammers,
Crowbars and spades those who crush'd the hill, their bones
Are scatter'd around roadsides!
To serve you they become laborers,
Coolis and porters,
Besmear'd with dust your burdens
They carry, they're human beings,

I sing for them! Stepping o'er their oppress'd chests
The new uprising emerges!
In three-stori'd house you sleep,
At the bottom we live,
And rever'd you as god! Expect that no more today!
Earth's loving essence saturates their soul and body,
Helm of world-boat they control, on my head I put
Dust from their feet, smear'd with dust
Together we walk on the street!
Anoint'd is my body with the blood of sufferers
Of the world, in the new morn a new red sun rises!
Break all the rust'd doors of the heart!
Remove the wrappers from skin paint'd!
Allow all frozen blue sky-air to gush into your chest!
Open all the bolts!
Let the sky fall down o'er our house! Let
The moon, sun and stars drop on our heads!
Let all human beings of all ages, of all countries stand
At one confluence to hearken
The melody of flute of one union!
With pain if one is inflict'd - equally it
Spreads o'er everybody's heart!
Showing disrespect to one is humiliation
To all, shame to whole mankind !

Today is the great uprising
Of the immense suffering of the noble mankind!
Up above god smiles,
Down here satan trembles!
[Shorbohara]

A few words:

In this poem the poet affirmed that the labor class people are weak and helpless in this world. They should not be treated unjustifiably as they belong to the weaker class of the society. Poet urged, let all human beings of all ages, of all countries stand at one place of union to listen to the melody of flute of one mankind.

A Complaint to God

Dust-smear'd helpless children beg thy requital,
Answer me, O God, the Father primordial!
With lamp of grief in eyes thy entire creation I roam around,
Inasmuch as I see, dumbfound'd, I'm content'd!
Thou art so Benevolent!
So much thou lovest us, so Majestic thou art!
God, O God!

O Lord, so beautiful is thine creation,
With so much greatness!
Sitting on the top of creation like an anxious mother cryest
Thou, no peace, no happiness thou hast,
Things thou dost crumble down
And create them again,
So inquisitive thou art! The sky thou dost
Cover with emerald-green—lest sun's blazing heat
Makes the eyes pale, thou dost blow thy wind
To soothe our scald'd heart!
God, O God!

Thy command the sun, moon and stars obey
At the dawn and dusk, the day,
Night, sky and air—
No one owns them alone; whatever
Exists in this world - flowers with smell, fruits
With juice, the pleasing earth, water and songs of birds—
Equal rights they share o'er them—'tis His command,
God, O God!

Yellow, black and white, mankind Thou hast creat'd –
'Twas thy wish! Black we're Thou knowest,
Fault's not ours! Sayest Thou not~ only in white's island
Shine the sun and moon!
Supremacy the white will show o'er others, ~ Thy law 'tis not !
The whole creation disobeys, shows Thee disrespect!
God, O God!

The earth— Thy youngest daughter,
Dust and soil Thou didst give her,
Holding the cup of milk on their mouths
She feeds her sons! Her happiness roams
Around like a pea-cock with spread-out feathers!
But not so happy her sons - greedy, they're satans!
In jealousy with each other they fight,
God, O God!

Pushing thee out Thy seat they occupi'd!
In this green earth Sahara, Gobi they creat'd!
Kings they become for a while –breaking the thrones
Graveyards they create their own!
Become they heroes when the food the snatch
From the mouth of their own brothers!
God, O God!

Like leech they suck blood,
They're the merchants!
The land they nurtur'd like own child,
But landlord they are not!
On the land ne'er they put their feet,
But becometh they land owners!

Those cheat and cunnings are stronger!
About wisdom and science the butcher talks
By mere mending his knives!
God, O God!
Powerful are nations for fighting war unjust!
Killing warrior-babies the shameless feels pride!
Trades' silver-wheel
Had squeez'd thy wheel,
What a shame! Unruly things thou dost
Tolerate, the Greatest thou art!
The oppress'd can hardly withstand,
Humiliation anymore they won't
Indulge, God, O God!

The drumbeatings all around,
Frighten'd they're not! The dying men send
The message of killings— "kill", "kill" !
Thou suck'd up whate'er blood left little,
In the bloodless body the bones fight the battle!
The bones broke not in hundred years, now singing ~
Triumphs for new uprising!
Triumphs for the oppress'd!
Triumphs for the God!

Together shall we enjoy this earth thou hast bestow'd
On us, the umbilical cord of the world link'd with the first
Day of creation! With palm-full of flowers and fruits
The world walks door to door! Any such robber exists
There to rip off my paddy that I stor'd?
The smell of life I find in the food
Of my hunger after so long a time, O God!

Thy gifts— light and rain pour down from the sky,
Who shoots from the sky,
Throws balloons up high?
Vast sky and the air a place of terror they made?
Thine endless boundary whose canons can guard?
Any remedy there? From the evils truth will be freed?
God, O God!
Which oppressor ties our hands that thou hast given?
Whose shackle of law obstructs my freedom of
    movement?
I have thirst, hunger, I have my life!
A human being I 'm, also a noble!
I control my tongue, my neck is straight!
My mind-shackle I've torn apart!
But my hand-shackle someone has pull'd
After a long time, O God !

Again the bow'd down heads are elevat'd up
In the sky! The slave is unti'd, the prison-wall he broke!
After a long time he lik'd the sky, air
And light around him, the salvage is sweeter
Than the prison life~now he realiz'd!
Resonates around a free voice of the free world—
Triumphs for the oppress'd!
Triumphs for new expedition!
Triumphs for new uprising!
[Shorbohara]

A few words:

The helpless poor people wanted the relief and salvage. They begged to God, Who is majestic and benevolent and the Lord of All. The world He created for all human being is the place of equality where color, race and religion should be merged in one point. The poet complained to God why people are committing crimes against humanity continuously in this world He created.

My Explanation

A poet I'm of the present-day, not a 'Prophet' of the future,
Poet or Poetaster, whate'er callest thou me I endure
That reticently! Someone says, 'In future thou wilt be
A pertinacious stubborn poet! Where's that eternal message of *Rabi*
In your poem, O Poet?' Blames me everybody,
Yet I sing only dawn's *Bhairavi*!

Frustrat'd are the poet-friends, heave a sigh
Of despair when they read my
Poems! They say, pushing the cart of rubbish of politics
A worthy turn'd into a worthless, he reads
No book, an inept he is,
His wife possess'd him completely~ says
Someone; a lousy becometh fatty playing cards in prison!
In prison thou wert not bad, there thou shouldst go again!

Says guru, now thou dost shave beard with sword!
In her saturday-letter my sweet heart
Castigates me, 'A good-for-nothing thou art!'
I say, 'Sweet heart, what if
I open thy guilt in public?'
Then and there to me she stopp'd
Writing letter! Abandoning everything I got marri'd,
But Hindu calls me, 'A Muslim in concealment '! I wonder
Whether I'm an unbeliever
Or a Muslim, which one suits me
Better *Tiki*, beard or *dhuti* !

All greedy *moulvis* and *mollahs* say angrily-'Speaks he always

About gods and goddesses,
Outcast this rascal from the religion! Here we
Issued the fatwa: He is an unbeliever *Kazi*,
Though a martyr he wants to be!
Conceit'd we're and vers'd in some chapters
Of scripture we share on others
Food!' Hindus think, in Farsi words he writes
Poetry,~ 'An inferior cur he is!'

New comers in non-violent movement and
The followers of non- cooperation
Are not happy too! Someone says,
I'm the 'violin of violence', I appease
The revolutionaries! 'He is non-violent', thinks
The revolutionary, 'If not, then why the song of wheel he sings?'
Fanatic Hindus consider me as an atheist,
A Confucian thinks I'm less-fanatic,
Swaraji thinks discontent'd I'm,
The others think~ a hassle to them!

Men think, I'm women-approaching!
Women think to them I'm antagonistic!
The friend lives in abroad- said, 'Thou hast not been
In England? 'What a shame, this much thy learning!'
'The sun of the new age!'~ Admir'd me my fans,
Though not a poet of epoch but as per the trend
Of the day I'm a poet, O my friend,
That makes me feel bad when I think! At ease
I sleep a lot putting the eyeglass on eyes!

What a dull, unintelligible trash I write,

Do I myself understand anything of that?
My hands rise not
High enough, so I keep my neck down while I write!
Friends, thou couldst not evaluate me but
The British ruler did!
Whatever I write, saying priceless
They pay me no price! 'Thou hast heard whistle
Blowing? Hoo-hoo~,the king's sentry
Is always after somebody?'

Friend! Thou hast seen me in my own
Mind-temple, exhaust'd I'm, fail'd to govern
My ill-fat'd captive mind! As oft I put it
In chain it tears the chain off, my mind I made
Crippl'd as I beat it again and again,
My mad-mind paid heed to none!
Not even to Rabi and Ghandhi!
Suddenly
It woke up, look'd for tiger all over the forest
In the darkness of night!

Spoke to myself, 'Crazy,
Listen, thou art now in a shape pretty!
Miss no more chance, becomest thou almost a leader,
Never wilt thou be a full leader!
'Fool, to shed tears on eyes spray now
Pepper powder while speakest thou
In a public meeting!Take chance, mend
The leaking roof of thy house,
Missing this opportunity thou wilt lament otherwise!'
Realizing not aught like a minstrel he sings
The songs and wanders around,

Listening to his songs they say- 'Nothing to be worri'd
About! His days he passes in chewing betel leaf and nut!'
No more epidemic of malaria, *Swaraj* came riding
A horse-coach, donation they need, they bring
Food for the hungry, the children cry, mother comforts—
'Be quiet! Look, here comes *Swaraj*!'

But the *Swaraj* the hungry baby wants not,
Wants little bit of rice, little bit of salt,
The day pass'd by, the baby ate no food, torments
Of hunger—hungry baby's stomach it burns!
I cri'd, rush'd out like a mad,
From my mind *Swaraj* was vanish'd!
I wept and said, 'Thou art still there, O God!'
They drinketh the baby's blood, ought to be humiliat'd!'

A whole burnt eggplant we brought, not the *Swaraj*-service,
Grabbing food from the mouths of hungry babies
They rais'd crores of money,
But *Swaraj* came not with money! No money in the hungry society!
A son it kills, snatching him away from the bosom of a mother,
We say, eat grass, O the tiger!
A mother I've seen begging for her dead
Son wrapping him with a cloth!

Friends! I can not talk anymore, this heart is fill'd with torments!
Having heard and seen so many things happen'd
Around me, irritat'd and angry I speak out
Whate'er comes in my mouth,

Blood alone I can not shed,
So I write the words smear'd with blood!
In utter distress, high ideologies, big words
Come not in my mind, my friends!
The eternal epic ye write, O my friends,
As ye are happy and affluent!

Care not whether die or live, this trend when
Fades away above my head Rabi will shine,
Many bright youths will come forward,
From the mouth of three hundred
Thirty million people
Those who snatch the morsel,
Pray to Lord—
May their destruction be written with my words
Anoint'd with blood!
(Shorbahara)

A few words:
As a person and as a poet he had to take false acquisition, stark criticism in his poetic life and personal life. This poem was written by the poet with vivid explanation to all those complaints and false acquisition that were directed to him from a corner of narrow minded people of the society he lived with.

The Graceful Young Man

No sooner had the *shefali* of autumn fallen down
And lotus-illumination of *ashwin* blown
Out than you heard the song of falling leaves–
The call of autumn from the flowers
All o'er, my friend! The falling *kamini* kiss'd your sleepless
Eyes, then came down in your eyes
The sleep of the nightly mysteries;
The fading lotus became your chaperone; under her feet
Your illusory girl trampl'd the *shephali* and appear'd
Through the snowy galaxy-garden!
There came the tears of autumn,
The flower-dropping dark foggy night;
The wet wind spoke to exhaust'd
Tamarisk tree in grief, the woods throbb'd and wept!
The tearful eyes of fog and shadows you saw, my friend,
In your estrang'd restless heart, a pain-inflicting insect
Enter'd that day! The cry appear'd not in eyes but in heart,
Took refuge in your heart that love without hope, words
    with broken
Tears! Friend, when the virgin *ashwin*
Of your life dress'd like a widow! When her
Petals of passion and glowing desire
Dropp'd from the garland of white rose– I knew not;
I knew not the night
Of separation smiles in your life, towards an unknown
Depth your journey just began,
O the stoic of the road, from which forest the abandon'd
Flute call'd you! We only know, tumbling down
At your feet she cri'd all the way,
She begg'd you!

Memory of your footprints she paint'd with a brush of dust!
In my mind many words are unfurled off and on! No more you're with us but
Here we came to feel the warmth of the footprints you left on the trail
You walk'd through, written are here many tales!

I know not wherefrom you hear my song, O the estrang'd Poet!
For which endless Sahara you walk alone beyond
The unending night of longing, beyond the moon,
Sun and stars in endless estrangement?
Those accompanying you in the road, call you from behind,
'O the friend of *shefali*, the lover of dew! O my friend,
With you take our memory of tears!'
What this side of shore tells you, do you hear?
Whispering words budge back and forth 'tween the shores!
In my mind whose sound I hear?
How far are you and where?
In hereafter or in the core of heart
You built a home far away from the sight?
While sitting in there words of heart you listen?
Neither you nor the sun, moon and stars got lost, my friend !...

That path, that intense memory of journey
Still exist, but not that romance, not that amity
To draw nigh to someone beloved—
No end, no beginning, no fatigue,
No satisfaction there I find—
The more I get the more I want!

That desire, that awesome attraction,
Those new expeditions in my orbit of imagination-
You snatch'd everything from me, my friend!
No more surge of laughter and happiness!
That little home with full of life is
Now empty, in the heart prevails emptiness!...
O the young! Endless
Is your vigor of life! Perhaps lost
We're not in this desert,
Perhaps with new identity you'll emerge,
Thankful you'll be with my gifts, so many words..
So many words were lost in the past, so many words will resonate!
In my mind it comes only—'Tis you only in flesh and blood
We want, the e'er-lasting message you brought in,
O the joyous hero, in my heart a pain still remains!
A silent cry of emptiness still roars,
In frustrations heart still murmurs!

Your message is the gift for everyone,
Pain is not there, my friend! When someone alone
Incurs loss, there is no solace, no peace! Friend,
Confidante, lover and brother we lost,
In poet's delight'd realm there exists no sorrows and pain,
In that realm let someone
In grief be happy! An artist, a poet you're that
They know, your rejuvenat'd life they drink not!

A wayfarer they saw, not the lord Krishna, he drown'd
Not in the lake, happy they are- on the bank
Of the lake they were still waiting!
To this day our heart is overcast,

We know not whether Krishna were an artist,
A story teller or a poet !
For our kith and kin we cry, we cry for dear ones,
In remembering Krishna we shed tears!
No sooner had our hope and words exhaust'd,
The hunger subdu'd, the amrit in the pot finish'd,
Our wishes fulfill'd than the harbinger arriv'd
At noon! All the thirst, desire cried out
Embracing the earth- they want not
To go, at the parting moment they were in grief,
Earth felt the stress! As if
The forest, water, wind and the land
Start talking! As though everyone began
To Urge -'go not there!'
Henceforth for this land and water the nature
Felt attraction so much ! Our heart
Was broken while they part'd- O My friend,
Still in our bosom we feel the blood-smear'd pain!

O the youthful, O the morning sun, O the graceful artist,
At noon with thirst tremendous you arriv'd near *Kailash*,
Saw her beauty, thirst you satiat'd by heavenly Ganges,
Thirsty again! You drift'd to other side of Ganges,
Or perhaps in the ear of tearful goddess
You dangle today as a red amaranth! O the ascetic!

O my wayfarer friend, O my love,
Wherever you live
Recall me with the memories
That I offered you as offerings
On the bank of weeping *Reva*! Being absorb'd
In the meditation of beauty those who came with pride

And valour of poverty, those who sacrificed,
Those who build not, but create,
O the Poet,
Their simple gesture just acknowledge
In this day of remembrance
The way in your life you accept'd them!

Actors they're not, nor are they the leaders of the country,
The gardens they built are empty,
They've heart, but no big arrangement, no tumults; and
Be happy with all those, O my friend in heaven!
Those who build palaces, honor is their due, crown they own!

In a short time their built-up palaces are collaps'd, unknown
They're, nation and man they create secretly!
Death angel garlands them who talk pompously
And brag for their vainglorious talk!
This 'today' is fake, but for how long?
An eternal throne the history and future
Can create, the world can put you there!
Though friends they're not today, but will be then –
No more offerings, today only they're in my remembrance!
[Shorbohara]

A few words:
In the poem the Poet himself is the graceful young man who is like a saint or a man or an incarnation of Lord Krishna. He is a lover, an artist and a poet. The poet hopes– those who create obstacles in the smooth-going society will be his friends one day.

The Ambidextrous (The Arjuna)

O fear not anymore, underneath the Himalaya the East rocks!
Penetrating the snows of mountain-peak the Ambidextrous gets
To his feet! Open'd his eyes the great ascetic came out
Ignoring the fatalities of 'the third age' of the world!
Stood up the hero of *Mahabharata*, and
Said, 'Here I am'. With youthful vigor the ancient East dances!

From eternity *Partha* came out of his incognito life,
Stain'd were countless arrows of *gandib* with blood like
Red lac dye! With running chariots *pancajanya* is blown
With shouting of soldiers, with the storm forests dance,
The *rasatala* swings,
With death the life giggles and dangles!

Through ages time and again the oblivious,
Sinful *Kuru* soldiers live and die, they're slaves
Of *Duryodhana*, controll'd by *Duhshasana*!
In *Lankakando*, in *Kurukshestra*,
In greedy demons' eyes, in gallows, in prison,
They're ever-known!
You thought,
Debt of oppression no one will pay off?

Ceaselessly rotates the wheel of time!
Today, we see them on the top of time
Emperor today though,
In prison he'll be morrow,

Killing occurs relentlessly in *Kamsa's* prison,
Nrishinha came out of prison but defeat'd again!

The one beaten by shoes, tomorrow he'll be rever'd,
Women prisoners behind bars for years welcom'd
With honor! Sound of drum-beat all around!
Shankara, the dread of the past arises! *Shita* is imprison'd,
The chaste of India, cri'd in the sea of *Lanka*,
Watch she will tomorrow cremation of *Ravana!*

Through ages appears warrior-chief in new forms, god as charioteer!
Through ages comes the singer of *geeta*, savior of the soldiers—
The righteous-*pandovas*! In evil pandemonium
Whenever died a chaste-woman
Projapati was then behead'd
By Shiva's sword!

Falgoni comes to initiate us with a new counsel,
Sleep no more, rise up all
Strong men! And listen not to fake message of peace,
Many *Dodhichi* offer'd their bones,
But the demon died not, freedom we want looming
Thread and wasting time in seating!
Rise up all strong men!
For weaving false loom suffer not in body the pain!

Shackle you tear with right hand, throw arrow with
The left on unarm'd prisoners, O the arm-bearing age!
Worshiping deity we got banana only!
Now you come O *Mahabali!*

On the front seat of chariot let
The wheel thrower be seat'd,
Rendering service for many days to the truth,
Any more we cannot bear its death!

There roars the cannon to kill mosquitoes~'The revolutionary we kill'd -
Our right hand is cuff'd, we kill mosquitoes with the left!'
Believing in superstitions like 'wall lizard'
'Or 'sneezing' we still live with *tiki* and beard!
Almost dead we're in our
Struggle to be alive there,
O the Ambidexter! In our hand give us something,
Let us die one more time to get a relief from this life!
[Fonimonosha]

A few words:

In this poem the poet encouraged the oppressed people that one day someone will come in India like the god Arjuna with ambidextrous power to defeat the oppressor. This leader can tear the shackle with one hand and throw arrows with the other to eliminate the oppressor. In this poem the poet urges the people of India to wake up leaving their superstitions, bigotry and religious hatred behind.

A Woman Prisoner In A Remote Island

The goddess of speech
Of India is yet to be releas'd,
For how many years in prison
She would be in that island?
Echo'd a cry above the altar—
'One hundred fifty years'....
Far away in the Andaman island the graceful
Lotus is fad'd away with cruel
Touch of steel batons, weapons of arm'd soldiers
Tore the lotus there into pieces!
Alas ! In presence of a sentry the composer
Sever'd the string of vina, a suppress'd melody of stringless sitar
Drift'd away from the island!
Is goddess free today? That secur'd city is destroy'd?
In the mud of devil's land the lotus is bloom'd?
In the heaps of cannon-shell shish-mohal is built?

Violent affrays are sanctifi'd with purity and peace
Amidst smell of blood? Then why aggriev'd offerings
Before a deity? Why's that sound of conch?...
Far away is the Andaman island!
There day and night the goddess works rigorously,
As a prisoner she husks paddy, oil of *Aroti*
You brought from that life-exhausting
Drudgery? Brought oil of sacrificial fire
For those brave sons?- Alas ! O the foppish worshipper !

In vain you blow the conch of goddess!
From the altar comes out only the cries !

O the worshipper, offerings you give to which
Deity? In India where is that free goddess of speech?
When the law is not the ruler there,
If truth I speak ever
Imprison'd and oppress'd I'll be, no right
I've to oppose oppression! Like incarcerat'd
Shita the goddess takes the floggings of injustice?
Her blooming lotus is nam'd as
Rebel! O the worshipper, with all offering-stuffs
Are you ready for offerings?

Being scar'd they keep lion in the cage,
Shoot bullets on tiger ! One day who knows
The lotus will be in prison! 'Tis the timbre
Of sacred verse of destiny resonates on her sitar!
On the lotus the rightly guid'd
King of new era put his feet?
Let it be so, offer that handful of adoration,
Play Krishna's conch! In the island
Amidst drudgery whirling
Of new age has begun!
[Fonimonosha]

A few words:
The British colonial government used Andaman and Nicobar as a penal colony, which was named 'Kalapani' or the Cellular Jail. Any one who was convicted of crime against the East India Company was sent to Andaman and Nicobar Islands with a life sentence: the convicts were forced to live in exile in the island.

Here in the poem the Poet depicted goddess Bharati or Bani as the goddess of speech. She was deported to Andaman Island as a prisoner. There she spent her days through hard labor and pain. Her chance to come back to main land was feeble, leaving the India a land without freedom of speech.

The True-Poet

Left behind was the falsehood,
Like a hero the truth mov'd ahead
Trampling the prison under his feet,
At the rising gate of morning sun that
Star of dawn proclaim'd
Its glowing victory with the sound
Of conch, 'tis the first beam kiss'd the facade
Of the sun of the morn, Oh! With gusty wind that
Radiant flame of rain is blown out!
The night is daz'd in the mid-sky, the universe
Is faint'd, profusely it rains in deep darkness, no stars,
Moon are awake now, bedimm'd are those lights,
In romping rivalry the billowy storm roars!

Kindling the candle of lightning of pain in this inclement
    night
Under dark sky who thou lookest for in the courtyard?
The candle blows out, kindling it again
Thou dost weep, as if the universe is being flogg'd by thine
Wailing! What fortune thou wantest?
Who art thou veil'd in blue clouds?
O dear, art thou Poet's green illuminat'd night?
What else thou canst take? Take a fistful of funeral ash!
Empty home, no more she is
There, no more! Faint'd mother
Is in a swoon, poet's lover
Is asleep, Swept away the funeral ashes
By the waves of Ganges !

Arriv'd in a palanquin of thunder that chaste lady?
A true mother of a true poet, like *Sharaswati*?
Crying for thee day and night dazzl'd are his eyes!
On farewell day he left his song in the voice of millions;
At length in a fit of pique he desert'd whole world amidst
Wailing! Looking upward with rais'd hands whom thou callest?
Refuge thou hadst taken in the pyre
Of crematorium, O mother, —
On the bank of the *Bhagiroti* river!

Mistaking it with morning star
Wayfarer ask'd the evening star—
'Where's the star that twinkl'd
In the mid-sky last night?'
Evening star at the horizon sadly looks,
Beckoning its beam it show'd the edge
Of the setting sky! Whose cloud-palanquin floats
Amidst wailing of clouds?
Whose screwpine-boat is tied on
The bank for ferrying across? In the land
Of saffron-color'd angels the eastern wind
Heav'd a sigh of frustration at the end of the golden
Kodomba forest! 'Tis a delirium! Never
Will he come back, only there
On the bank of the Ganges our wailing
Will wander around!

Written are the words in glowing crimson
Hue in a brush painting, blooming
Flowers smile in the green of garden,
Till today the pearl-casket fill'd with pollens and holy water,

With the melody of bamboo-*vina* the earth shivers
With cooing of cuckoos and peacocks,
Flar'd up the sacrificial fire and colorful clouds,
From the bridal-chamber of fire - *Hashantika* ridicul'd
And smil'd!
For whom all those lively festivals!
Illusions and falsehood everywhere, truth is immortal,
And turn'd into ashes! No more mistake! Exists
Only the voidness in space,
On the day of creation there
Only the truth was delineat'd forever!

With a victorious-flag on his shoulder the unbending
Conqueror of time will humbly return,
Being absorb'd in his own creation he left
When the call came from the capricious fate !
O the poet of epochs, thou didst die not of that death!
Manifest'd was the truth,
The graceful god in poet's voice!
The words are not echo'd, the songs
That not yet sung will fill up the world again,
'Tis true, not a lie! O we doth understand,
But defeat'd and scar'd,
We think and think only—whate'er
Is lost, lost fore'er!

No more there today the shrieking and wag-tailing
Dance of cuckoo, which eden-forest will incite it to dance again?
When about thee I think
Tears roll down my cheek,
O the bless'd poet,

The sanctifying! In such a time thou hast left
Us when India needs hundreds like thee, the heat
Of the scorching sun, a burning comet thou wert!
O the brave, garland'd with thorny cactus, adorn'd
With jewels thou hadst appear'd
With a whip of lightning in thy hand!
With a fascinating look those fallen *Bangali*
Had stared at thee!
In thine bugle-horn tingl'd the sonorous sound-
'The God is Great, not the evil, triumph for mankind!'

Slavery thou didst not accept, nor didst thou ruin self-respect,
God is true, ever-awakening, never to others' feet
Thy truth has bow'd down, no chastisement touch'd thee!
Alone hadst thou beaten the battle drum deafeningly
In the crowd of fame-mongers,
Blind, fake and cowards!
In the midst of the spurious people till death
Thou hadst surviv'd as a true poet,
As dust thy body has return'd to dust,
But not thy truth! Never without sufferings
A country woke up; in the gathering
Thou wert the horn blower of goddess
Of peace!

Who will waken up the people?
Where's that truthful soul?
Neglecting us our God we humiliate! Flute,
And bugle-horn thou hast taken from us, left
Are only broken drums and instruments,
Our smile to appease others is hidden in tears!

Hanker'd thou wert not after fame and honor, thou hadst learn'd
Not fake hospitality nor hadst thou dishonor'd
The honorable one, thou wert not
A door-keeper of the king, thou hast
Consider'd oppression as oppression
But not as kindness! Bow'd down
Not to shackl'd foot nor hadst
Thou surrender'd to intimidation, thou art
Inflexible, the fierce volcano with fire within;
Cowards' birthplace thou hast made pleasing!
O the great reticent, in death bed
Thou hast swallow'd silence's geniality and
Said goodbye. Our deceitful songs
Thou hadst not taken with thee! No murmuring
Of grief spread'd o'er at thine
Demise! How graceful thou art! The rain
Dropeth down in heaven,
Lightning dazzles, the virgins bring
Down that pouring of rain whole night long,
Nobody awakes; clos'd are all doors of hut,
Only a wailing of a mother reverberates all over for her son lost!

At night wearing white cloth an ill fat'd widow wanders
In the crematorium, thinks- who kindl'd the fire in the pyre,
Remov'd her *sindur* from the head!
O God!
How couldst thou witness the agony
Of those two women? Their curse might inflict thee!
[Foni Monosha]

A few words

In the poem the poet represented himself as a true-poet who was never afraid of telling the truth, who trampled the falsehood under his feet and kindled the light of truth and justice. Though the poet was garlanded with thorny cactus but adorned with jewels and appeared with a whip of lightning in his hand to defeat the falsehood.

The Departing Song
Of The Truthful

Unknowingly the vivacious son of the goddess
Came here when he was lost,
O on this bank of Ganges !
The perplex'd mother found her lost son
O on this bank of Ganges !
In bamboo *vina* the wandering minstrel infus'd his melody,
Jingling sound he produc'd in its strings!
He finish'd not his song, call'd him by nick-name
Someone from the setting gate, delight'd he was!
O on this bank of Ganges!

O ! Listen, in such a stormy day some ruinous call'd him!
Poet's horn-bugle growl'd again, no melody was play'd in the flute,
The scorch'd eyes are fill'd with tears, in one stormy night
I recall opium-flower made this wound'd bird to sleep!
O on this bank of Ganges!

From homely attachment he freed himself
Since he is ever boundless!
That rhythm-crazy swinging with mother earth!
Oh! Ablaz'd with fire he offer'd us light,
Offer'd ambrosia withstanding torments of poison!
At the blazing pyre pain-inflict'd-rebel found peace at last!
One more time at the bottom of the green tree
With a new vina he will appear
O on this bank of Ganges!

[Foni-Monosha]

A few words
At the end of the life the flute of the truthful rebel poet rendered no melody. Withstanding torments of life he offered us light and amrita to drink. Though he took rest in peace but one day he will appear with a new vina in his hand at the bottom of a green tree with new hope and aspirations.

The Song of Universal Solidarity

Rise up all the prisoners on hunger-strike,
Rise up all ill-treat'd, ill-fat'd of the world!
With rumbling of thunder the voice emanates today amid all
Oppression from the bottom of the heart of the oppressed
  people,
O with new birth
There comes the unique earth!

All primordial fetters, scriptures and rituals
Caus'd the devastation, we'll
Break them now! Breaking the huge prison
The have-nots come out, none
Will be there to bow down!

Chorus:
O on the new foundation new world will be built!
Listen! O the tyrants!
Listen! O the hoarders!
The have-nots we were,
Ever-conqueror
We will be, O in this last fight,
Stand up with your rights!
Again in this world the mankind will be
Reawakened through this song of universal solidarity!
[Foni-Monosha]

A few words
The poet put forward an awakening song of solidarity for all oppressed people of the world to wake up and lay a new foundation of the new world to establish the rights of the oppressed.

The Harbinger

O the harbinger, can you walk through the infest'd
Hovel of ruffians and rascals there and safeguard
Yourself while passing through it? Can you penetrate
That circle of battle line? Ripping apart
The rock will you rise up like a big tree? Over
The life's dumping ground vultures
And kites fly! O the glorious baby, there
What expedition can you make? In this ugly game of throwing
Stones and spattering muds! Besmearing
Face anoint'd with black dye like people
In *Bhojpuri* village fair, the Bengal
Has become frenzi'd? The sun has forgotten his meditation?
Frantic outcry in wine-shops brought down
Indra and *Borun* to the earth? O the anxious
Front-traveller, what message you have for us?
Slanderers' drum beat will stop? Can I hearken unto your mystic words?

Slanderous chorus song
The men and women sing,
They think, for the triumph of allurement 'tis their ovation !
Know you aught of the horse rider of neo-revolution?
All darkness end'd, the east-ward door was open?
Here corner'd was an intellect by the intrigue of many! The *Joban*,
The unbelievers drive him from behind!
Anyone of new generation here to save him? Anyone bereav'd,

Dust-smear'd, half-nak'd?
The temple and mosque the satans made their
Conference place, O the harbinger,
The *Jhat* and *Kalapahar* will turn up
To destroy those satans' counseling hubs?
Give us that tidings – hemm'd in contract'd belief still flutter
The flags of religion knott'd with *tiki* and beard!

In the slanderers' *Brindaban* I want not to sing any song,
I dislike watching the degrading humiliation
Of beauty! Within my heart sobs my furious message with anger
And pain, today in drunkard's liquor-shop *binapani* becomes the dancer!
Those demons— greedy and selfish churn
The lives of people, shares they distribute among
Them for profits, when poison is churn'd out their trace I find
Not! In the ashes of dead, in crematorium I look for the god
Of destruction! His eyes are clos'd for
Smoking marijuana! O the harbinger, O the explorer
Of youthful-minds in wilderness!
Where is my sword of the new age?
[Fonimonosha]

A few words:
The Poet assailed the evil elements of the society and appeared as harbinger who can salvage the falling society from the evil hands.

The Battle Between Hindu-Muslim

Fear not! After a long time in India the life is back, rejuvenat'd
Are the graveyards and crematoriums! The dead
Or wound'd woke up with pain!
Khaled gripp'd the sword, *Orjun*
Throws arrows! India woke up, there
With bamboo-sticks Hindu-Muslim fight each other!

Dead are Hindus, Muslims are kill'd! Those who liv'd
Are dying now, no shame in such a death!
A spirit has arisen, so the fighting began!
Today is the test – who is more ardent—
In face to face battle tomorrow— to die
Or not to die!

Hearken to the din of life in the voice of faint'd,
They rise up instantly! Uproars have begun!
Stop not churning up the strength! Infidels and
Jobons woke up! Hindu and Muslim rise again
With prowess! You woke up,
God woke up,
God is in action
As per His plan!

'Tis is a test of strength 'tween the trainer
And his deciple! Fearlessly they're
Slaying the timid India. Time watches whether wrist
Or fist is slic'd off by a mild strike,
Who won in the killings, who won the battle! Which 'soldier' lost

Not his sense in 'the mock-fight'!
Which 'hero' wraps him up, pulls the quilt
Watching few drops of blood!
In fear he left the sword, he is in rampant
Delirium! Oh! In coming days leaders of the revolution
Will be those weak-mind'd!
Seeing mere whirling wind they get faint'd!
What if approach a cyclone or a storm?
God tests them –in the sea of blood who can swim?

Your own temple and mosque you demolish'd,
That foundation was laid by the people who're subjugat'd!
As if God himself destroy'd his houses! With sacred
Clay free people will build
Martyrs' altar, temple's dome is shatter'd?
Oh! now you sleep too in the temple that is shatter'd!

Who kills whom, in darkness there prevails suspicion,
Unknowingly in the darkness he kill'd his kin own
Mistaking with an enemy! With the retreat of suspicion sun will
Rise, no more narrowness, vision will be perceptible!
No more will they watch
A brother beats his own brother in such!
Those three-prong'd rods and swords
Inflict'd the destiny of India with wounds!

The rod that demolish'd the tomb and
Dome will smash the enemy-fort tomorrow morn!
In the morn no more fight 'tween the brothers,
Enemy and the kin they'll recognize!
They fought but woke up now

Any how!
Hoist the flag of triumph! If your tail is burnt then
Golden *Lanka* you can burn!
[Fonimonosha]

A few words:
Poet always condemned the bigotry and communal hatred that existed in the communities of Hindus and Muslims in India. This poem is written satirically. The poet described the rampant fight, vandalism and killings that took place between the two ignorant fanatic groups.

The Sea

[The first wave]

O the sea, O my friend,
The insatiable, the ever-estrang'd!
Which pain has spark'd thee to swell up to the brim?
Something thou wantest to say? And to whom,
O my friend?
Blue sky above, shore below longing for thee!
Speak out, O the restless breaker, tell me
In thy heart why so much murmurings
Of the waves? Why's this unending rumbling?
Thy endless crying stopeth not for even a day or a night,
O my friend! Tell me what ails thee in thy heart?
Someone thou hast lost and when? Who was in thy dream?
That illusory auspicious girl? Where doth she live?
Dost thou behold her? Why is she dissociat'd from thee,
Whom thou lovest so much! Had she
Been here? Her feelings are hurt?
Her face she doth hide in the hair of dark night?
Alone sleepeth she in a moon-lit bed? Hence to arouse
Tidal waves the moon attracts so much
Of thy liveliness? In moon hidden is thine secret?
Tell me, my friend,
tell me—Is it the song? Is it the wailing?
Is it the furious water-rippling?
Is it thy growling? That moon, thy belov'd?
Hiding behind clouds lives she far far away? That spot
In the moon~ a spot of passionate kiss?
That's why away she lives!
Is it her anger? Or affection?

Knowest thou that?

And so grudgingly on the waves in vain
Thou smackest thyself? As if an eternal man
Thou art absorb'd deeply in thy own
Dream! Unruly but quiet thou art, Knowest no one
But thyself! No waves there; even a ripple yet to begin!
Like a big mirror thou art translucent, calm, resting
Her face on thy face the shore sleeps! The ascetic, the meditating!
There appear'd the moon— when, thou knowest not,
As if bewilder'd thou art!
O the reticent,
In profound admiration thou hadst spoken out—
'Graceful, what a graceful!'
Singing with thee universe woke up, 'Graceful, what a graceful'!
That archaic word, that primordial saying!
'Tis the pain for being in seclusion O the king,
Thou hast understood~ a lonely becometh elegant
When he's coupl'd!
Moon appear'd in the heart or in the sky~ knows no one,
Not a soul will know, remain unknown
For-ever. After so long a time laden
With loneliness thou feelest as if
Everything's empty!
Someone wants me, something is not there,
Whomever I find~ more deeply I want her!

There arose happiness and sorrows,
Arose tidal waves,
Swinging began, waves broke the shore, rampant thou wert,

The trembling sleepy land cri'd out!
In despondence drifts along thy breath in the air!
In the endless sky joyful outburst of blue emerg'd there!
In astonishment came out all newly creat'd stars,
Thrill'd was the earth; grass, flowers,
Fruits sprout'd out from within her bosom! Light and air
Emanat'd with invigorat'd life, all over
The known and unknown places
A song amazing drift'd across!
What an excitement! O dear, what a tumult!
So many hearts, so much of love!
Breeze swips over branches of trees, how intimate they're!
On their way the waves entwine each other,
Flowers and bees in passionate kiss– daylight
Doth plummet on earth! Delight'd
Everyone ~talking,
Making hue and cry and singing!

O my friend, my sea-king! In thy dream appear'd
A charming face, thou hast woken up, pain thou feelest in
    thy heart!
With passion and pain heart melts down, nerves tear apart!
O the sea, the curious, the eager— thou swellest
Up with the euphoria in sorrows and happiness!
As if a deep disgruntl'd shadow fell upon thee,
Blue was thine transparent body!

The sea, O my friend!
With excruciating anguish thou hadst grumbl'd!
On thy waves of desire dropeth the shadow of thine
Belov'd again and again!
On the waves her shadow breaks, brings attachment!

The endless covertness is yet to over,
Thou cryest, I cry, cries the time! The summer
Cries, monsoon cries, cry the spring and winter!
All night long I hear that song
Of wailing, my friend,
With thee cries the estrang'd
Universe, O the sea! Thou cryest, I cry, cries my belov'd!
O my lonely friend,
Tears in thy eyes tumble down!
With same agony and pain thou cryest,
I cry, cries my belov'd!

The Sea

[The second wave]

O the sea, my friend, my rebel!
In which pain thou art frenzi'd with indomitable
Amorous sport in each wave pattern off and on?
O the frantic, why this dancing?
Why flauntest thou in futile grudge?
Throwest thou on the edge
Of shore? O the all-devouring! The earth thou grabest
Bit by bit with extreme hunger! O the restless! Thou wantest
Not the earth in rest, O the dance-oblivious!
The earth swings high above thy waves!
O the fickle, perturb'd! Again and again
Thou pullest the *anchal* of the horizon
Girl! *Herem*-concubines, the pearl
Girls are awaiting her arrival,
O the amusing!
Seems endless thy amusement! In futile something
Thou lookest for in the shore! Whose footprints!
Mistakenly on thy shore walk'd someone at night!
She, ingeniously conceit'd! All tears thou droppest at her feet,
Reluctantly she smil'd at thee! Thy kiss she ignor'd,
Resist'd thee with her conch bangles! ~She left!
Keep searching her with the boat
Of desperation, in the growling of waves thou cryest—
'My belov'd, O dear belov'd!'

Tell me, why so much virulence, so much burning in chest?

Who requit'd not thy love? Who tore thy garland?
Oh! That boastful girl retain'd that much beauty,
That much life! O the sea, she insult'd thee!
O *Maznu*, who's that *Laili* so madden'd
Thou art for love? O the sea-king, the bewilder'd, the estrang'd!
Who's that princess for whom thou hast revolt'd?
Today abducting that King's daughter
Whom thou wantest to defeat in the battle, thy lover?
Adorn'd with the turbans of sea-foam in groups
Thy army of waves march forward in rows,
With hasty command moves thy general in the front,
Fly there the balloons of clouds, stealthy under-sea mountain--
Thy sophisticated 'mine'!
Sharks, crocodiles, whales are thine 'submarines'!
Fishes are thine naval force! Riding walrus
Thou shovest like a hero, the frantic, the restless!
Being a victorious when wilt thou bring thy belov'd?
That she will come, pearl-garland
They make at sea bottom! The corals doth string red
Garlands! O the sea ! O my friend,
When the night of illumination will come for thy bride?
For her the newly creat'd
Islands pleasure gardens they build!

On thy bosom floats the sea-vessels like thy pet pigeons!
Thy dangling waves caress the birds, make them dance,
O the turbulent! O the tender!
Water gushes up there
With thy passionate outburst,
On her beak thou dost

Kiss? Thy hope, the greedy vulture doth
Fly o'er, thy rope of hope the shore pulleth!
As if fly so many nameless birds in thy dream! Sometime
Becomest thou listless, wantest to hide!
To which remote land thou driftest
Down with low-tide?
As if hiding thyself feelest thou secur'd!—
Fatigu'd boatman sings *Bhatiali*, mind drifts along—
Far away towards an endless, goalless destination,
Thou floatest, the boatman doth float,
In the waves I float!

A lost one thou art, without destination!
Hearkening to someone's call silently walkest thou alone
Towards downstream? Dost thou hear the call from within heart?
Who cries in seclusion, beg for thy heart?

Finding not her anywhere thou lookest into thy own
Soul with shame— with pain— in humiliation!

Then, O the mighty man! Realizing mistake swellest
Thou up in high tide, breakest all the banks around, blowest
The horn-bugle and sayest:
'Love maketh no one weak, maketh someone
Glorifi'd!' To wine girl thou dost urge, 'Darling, a cup of wine!'
In deep sorrow it makes thee happy, makes thee forget
All torments! Like poison the pain of heart
Becometh froth in the mouth! O Shiva, the mad!
In thy throat holdest thou pain, that deadly poison!

O confidante, O friend!
After so long a time we met—
The two fugitives!

For thee so many words, so many songs,
So many pains to let thee know~ O the sea, my friend!
My friend, together we sit face to face,
Together we enter, thou holdest me with thy waves,
But no waves, only endless blue! Tell the whale to sit by the door,
So that sun and moon enter not there,
We talk, only thou, me and our pain will be there!
Beneath the water we will not talk,~
If we talk, would be very brief,
'I'm estrang'd,
Thou art too, O my friend!'

The Sea

[The third wave]

O my hungry friend, the thirsty, so much water holdest
Thou in thy bosom, yet thou hast the endless thirst!
At thy feet tumbl'd many rivers~ big and small,
O the hungry! Still thou art insatiable!
O the eclipse, turbulent, thou hadst devour'd
Three-fourth of the earth!
No more wine~ with an empty glass
In hand the wine-girl trembles!

O the impassable! Open, open, open the door!
Stand by there at the door
The mountains and gorges,
With palm-full of offerings of fruits and flowers
The green earth and crops
Worship thee! O the valorous!
In thy own-self, in thy own waves,
Deeply absorb'd thou art,
Many painful songs of earth thou hearest not,
Seest thou the present and past, thou wilt
See the distant future~
O the saint, the stoic, the immortal observer!
Birth, death, sorrows and happiness
Rise and break on thy bosom like waves,
Delightfully thou watchest them always!

Earth bathes in thee every day O the sanctifi'd,
Still beautiful, still unfad'd like a flower just bloom'd!
O the sympathizer! Sins and agonies of the world

Thou wipest out!
To the earth thou comest down through clouds –
Thy loving daughter! Smiles she in the grasses and crops,
From her black eyes happiness dropeth down!
By being the streams thou dost cruise along,
Offerest so many colorful benefactions!

Thou dost break, build and swing~in endless amusement
with thy daughter! O the vast, thou hast no waning,
no decay, all waning thou hast fill'd up with new gifts!
O the graceful! Around the waist thou holdest
The earth like girdle of sapphires and emerald!
Incomparable swaying thou dost manifest with
Hip~swaying of the earth!

Friend! Like wine thy endless youth froths up in waves!
Many mermaids entice thee, many garlands
Dried up, dropp'd at thy feet, O the stoical!
But turnest thou a blind eye to them, as if all
The time in dreaming someone thou art engross'd!
With sedating herbs the demons robb'd
The city of gems, they had stolen the horse of Indra~
Thy sweet girl, they pilfer'd the amrita,~
Thy life! Everything's gone, left there only the murmur of waves,
Agonies and memories
Of excruciating pain!
Up above, down below, voidness is all around,
In endless wailing the vast stream bemoans!

O the great, O the ever~estrang'd!
O the sea, my rebellious friend!
O my graceful! I salute thee!

Take my salute!
O impenetrable! Thou hast the shore,
But exists there
No shore but the endless
Separation, exist only the dream and mistakes!

At the parting time no more
I'll be there,
In thine roaring waves
I wish my cry blazons!
In vain thou lookest for me,
O my friend ! O my sea!
Up to the brim thou art not,
Me too! Nothingness is all around!
In endless wailing
The stream bemoans in the middle !
(Shindu-hindol)

A few words:

The Poet completed this long poem 'The Sea' in three different epics– the First wave, Second wave and Third wave while he was in Chittagong (a port city of Bangladesh) in the year 1926. Those First, Second and Third wave were written on 27th july, 31st July, and on 2nd August 1926 respectively.

He addressed the sea as his friend and described him as a symbol of estranged lover whose heart is full of pain, like rumbling waves he swells up, on the shore he crushes with growling grudge and concealed anger. He is hungry and thirsty for love. Though he is indomitable and graceful but at the same time he is estranged and bereaved as his lover left him for ever alone.

My Secret Lover

Since I found thee not in my life,
Therefore to this day, O my queen, thee I love!
Sea in the middle, from both sides we whisper!
Here I'm, thou art there,
In the middle weeps the obstacle of expanse!
By being the shadow of forest thou dost beckon
Me, by being a desert
Thy shadow at all I behold not!

Each other by name we know,
Yet to be acquaint'd we're though!
In my chest the hope cries,
Fear in thine! On me wind of clouds
Doth create waves, dash against
Thy feet, on thy shore smash not
My waves, erod'd was my shore,
But not thine any more!

O my friend, to discern thee intimately time I had
Little, for a while on the tree a singing bird I settl'd,
My songs thou wilt recall when
I fly away, no bird but its songs will remain,
I will fly, weep thou wilt again,
O the shore of pain!

When my waves doth strike thy shore,
No one knows, O the unknown! No one will ever!
When I fly if dropeth on thy path a feather,
Pick it up by mistake, put it in thy hair!
Scare not,

Eventually thou wilt take it out!

In a morn of monsoon-downpour
Wilt thou shower
On me with thy lonesome mind?
O the screw pine flower of the wild!
In thy imagination wilt thou kiss on my mind-bottom
In deep night? Thou wakest up having a dream,
Thinkest so many things! With clouds criest thou,
O my crest'd cuckoo!

O my distant lover ! I bemoan for being alone!
No trace of shores! In the sea the waves dangle!
Melody of the flute would stop if I find thee!
Death could come! An alienation fill'd me
As I miss'd thee, prevails there the voidness in the heart
Of bamboo-flute, in the true flute the melody will be play'd!

Friend, not nearer to me thou art, stayest
Thou far away, but to my heart more nigh thou art!
In the shadow of a moon-lit night
Like an illusion thou shalt wait!
Sweetness lies in confidentiality— thou dost
Not talk to me, so what?
With me thou sleepest not,
In my eyes thou sleepest!

O my dream-thief, my secret!
That we're alive, 'tis my delight!
Where art thou, my queen! 'Tis needless to know,
Do I have to!

Loving thee— content'd I'm— I want not
To stay awake, let drowsiness in my eyes persist!

To love thee my lone sleep prompts my heart,
Shroud'd me a pain of loneliness, inebriat'd
With sorrows my heart will live long,
Thy moon-like face I'll portray from my vivid imagination!
In my sleep and in my awakening thou wilt
Remain, 'tis my pleasure ultimate!
From afar thou wilt listen to my song I'll sing!
If I stop singing thy pique will make me to sing!
An artist, a poet,
I'm, thou art my paint'd portrait,
My epic, my lyrics thou art!
From thee I want naught –
Thee I confer my gifts with content!

Where in thy heart liveth the estrang'd distant lover?
No need to know! No one finds the bottom there
Of a bottomless ocean! In concealment thou comest
Down in my epic, in my love, I breathe with that
Bliss, need to scour
Around for thee in the shore?
A distant-bird I'm, sing with zest,
But build not a nest!

In parting time if I receiv'd not any gift from thee,
That matters? Recall me
Thou wilt not ~ in thy mind,
In thy forgetfulness thou wilt
Recall me, again
Into my oblivion

Thou shalt appear, sweet heart,
I would be rejuvenated!
Even though thee I miss'd,
Unwaveringly I look'd
At thee, and
For thee many songs I sang!
(Sindhu-hindol)

A few words:
The poet is alone and his beloved sweet heart is somewhere far away. She is concealed bodily from him but not from his heart. He cannot reach her, he is estranged, bemoaning and bereft. In between them there only exists the expanse of vastness of the sea. He sings many songs for her and hopes one day she will appear again in his life. She will recall him in her forgetfulness that would rejuvenate him.

This poem was written on 28th July 1926 when the Poet was in Chittagong,

Bangladesh.

My Lover Without A Name

Thee I adore my dream-companion, my belov'd!
The arouser of thirst thou art in my heart
For not having thee! Thee I adore
O my fanci'd frolicsome lover,
Eternal youthful belle, my perpetual companion!
Thee I adore O my lover without a name! Accept my adoration,
My love...my secret stroller, O the lover fore'er!
Since the day of creation cryest thou hiding behind desire,
Thou didst not surrender,
Altruistic lamp of thine is yet to be kindl'd in a lightless
Home! O the infinite! comest thou not at the finite edge!
In my dream I find thee and lose thee in my dream again,
O the formless! as a sensual desire thou hadst come in my mind
Not as a chaste in my home! In my love thou hadst appear'd
As a lover not as a wife in my lips! By being the pleasing wine
Thou art conceal'd in grapevine
But not in my cup! Cries out my desire uncontrollable –
'Take off thy veil.'
My distant lover! Stay in distance, love me— come not
Nigh unto me. A blownout light
Thou art not nor a flame,
Nor art thou a mirage,
Thou art lustrous!....

Through generations in hereafter thee I offer'd *Arati*,
Hundred times again and again the same I offer thee!
Where'er any splendor I saw, ~ I ador'd it for thy sake, my dear!
In every magnificence and beauty I look'd there

For thee, O the amazing! The more I lift up the screen of wind,
More it increases! Thou weepest in estrangement,
Appear again and again like a rainbow,
The angel of sky, my charming dear! Though
Tri'd to reach thee— far away in horizon thou hadst
Disappear'd, my pain-inflicting queen, thou hadst not
Come, but I had thy word!

O fore'er distant lover, O the not-e'er-coming!
A disappointing hope of finding
Thee nearby me took me from planet to planet!
With the zeal of desire—I was born in this world,
Will be resurrect'd in the hereafter! In my overwhelm'd bosom
I've insatiable youthful passion,
Extreme desire, so birth I take again and again,
Worship anything I'm depriv'd of!..Whate'er is graceful
I kiss'd, when I kiss'd it became elegant, in all
Those things thy delightfulness I felt!
Tilottoma, slowly, very slowly thy lips I touch'd!
In the lips of every girl that secret reveals when thee I kiss'd!

When someone kiss'd his lover breaking her sleep in the morning,
In her drowsiness when she fell asleep for staying
Awake in the night, I kiss'd thee as if on every body's lips I kiss'd,
O the universal lover, my belov'd!
Along with passion of animals, birds, trees and creepers
My desire arises, amorously I dally with the universal desire!
Those who are depriv'd of love, enjoy pleasure
With their consorts—I'm one of them! primordial desire

When arous'd in the heart of god *kama* with the
Creator that day thou hadst come, to thee
I came alone. I was *Kama*, and thou wert *Rati*.
To the hearts of the youths
Access unprecedent'd we've henceforth!

What thou art and what not, I think and
Think, look around for thee! Didn't I look for thee in vain
With name and without a name? Futile
Was my love for thee,
For nothing everyone doth love me?
Confusing with someone thee I embrac'd,
She walk'd away! Why it happen'd,
Ah! Why it cometh to my mind—
Someone secretly loveth me more than I lov'd
My lover, She is more graceful— sweetest!
Becoming a new bride smile thou dost in my bride's heart.
Alas! Whome'er I find in my heart,
In her heart alone thou cryest,
O the rival of my lover!..many times—again and
Again it crosses my mind~
No, 'tis not that she! O the obscure, the indistinct!
Where art thou? Shall I meet thee? Thou wert
born or thou wilt emerge as a new born?
Talk to me, talk to me, my darling!
O my depriv'd-thirst arouser
Of love for e'er!

Thou wilt not talk? Today in my mind it cometh as usual~
Love is true, prevails forever, perpetual
He is not who doth love, he who is born in passionate
Desire grows up like a wish tree, branches it

Spreads out as if it sucks the life from air.

The sky is cover'd with the wings of green crane of desire!

Love's true, lovers are many- uncountable,
True love I want, I found ample,
Still my heart weeps in pain!
Wine's true, not the cup of wine,
Drinkest thou from whate'er
Cup, thou wilt be intoxicat'd, O my companion for-e'er!
After a long time I came to know thee,
And asham'd extremely!
Conceal'd thou art in my love, in vain I wept and look'd
    for thee
Through generations! O the incomparable! In thine every
Form thou callest me, I know thee,
Whome'er I love, she is thou! Thou wilt love me!
Love is one, lovers are many, that love
I drink pouring into many cups --
That wine elixir!
O the nameless, thee I drinketh from a pitcher,
From a glass, sometime from a cup with many desires!
[Shindu-Hindol]

A few words:
The name of his sweetheart is meaningless to him. The nameless beloved is poet's dream companion, his perpetual companion. She is concealed in his love. Her love, the elixir he drinks, pouring into many cups with many desires.

Note: The Poet wrote this poem when he was in Chittagong (the port city of Bangladesh) on 27th July 1926.

In remembrance of a parting time

O my friend, 'tis not just to meet someone
On the street, 'tis not the street conversation!
'Tis not just a casual touch of a hand
With someone's hand
That ends up suddenly in a street promenade!

With new identity in our heart
Thou hadst steadily appear'd
Not as a conqueror— but as a friend thou hadst
Come, smilingly our heart
And mind thou hadst plunder'd!

Occupying a throne a king thou wert not,
King thou hadst become while thou wert
In our heart, hence in this parting time more than
Us the pain thou hast taken!

In our million broken hearts live thou wilt ever as a pain,
Our next of kin thou hadst become with thine
Enduring identity— we'll meet thee again,
'Tis not just a street conversation!
[Shindu-Hindol

A few words:
Poet was in the mind and heart of the people. At the time of his parting from them he will be remembered as their next of kin, as their friend, as their king who occupied the throne of their hearts. His acquaintance with them was not momentary

like walking leisurely with someone in the street that ended up suddenly.

This poem was written when the Poet was in Hugli (India), dated: Kartik, 1332 BD. October, 1925.

Poverty

O poverty, thou hast made me great!
Christ's honour thou hast bestow'd
On me, adorn'd me with crown
Of thorns!—
O the ascetic, an appalling courage thou hast
Given me to speak out unhesitatingly, an insolent
Nak'd look, razor-sharp words;
Thy curse turn'd my *vina* into a sword!

Thy unbearable heat, O the proud ascetic, made
My gleeful heaven an insipid abode,
My beauty, my delight, my life,
Untimely thou hast dri'd up!
Whene'er I wanteth to take my palm-full of gift of beauty,
Comest thou forward and drinkest it, O the thirsty!
As my utopia the barren desert I behold there,
On my own beauty my eyes showereth fire!

Like a white *shefali* my painful-pale-desire wants
To bloom with fragrance spreadeth around.
Thou art cruel, thou breakest
Petal-stalks, branches of trees
Like a wood cutter!
In pity my heart fills with tears
Like an *ashwin* morning, like a tremulous
Humid earth! Thou art
The sun, thy heat blots out
The piteous dew! In earth's shadow more pallid I become!
Shatter'd is my dream, dream of beauty, dream
Of well-being! Pouring poison into thy throat thou sayest:

'In divine drink what's the benefit?
No burning, no inebriety, no madness! O the frail,
In this grief-striken world practising spiritual
Austerity is not thine penance!
Thou art the *Nag*, born with blazing pains!
Sitting in the garden of thorns
Thou wilt string flower-garlands, and
A mark of pain I adorn'd on thy forehead!'

I sing and string garland,
In my throat burning of poison
I feel, the *Nag-* and *Nag* girl there
Bit me all o'er!...

For begging alms thou roamest around, O the saint,
The unforgiving *Durbasha* ! A happy night
Spendeth the bride and bridegroom, speakest
Thou to them harshly~'Ignorant! Listen,
This world~ not the place of pleasure for anyone,
Here prevails indigence and sorrows, thorns lie underneath
The bed, around lover's arm, ' so enjoyeth!'
Instantly bewailing starts all o'er blissful heaven,
Light blows out quickly as if the black night will never end!

On his way walk'd a hungry lean body– seest thou,
Contract'd suddenly thy eyebrows, furious eyes threw
Arrows of fire! Epidemic, famine and storm
Struck the kingdom,
Burnt were all gardens of pleasure,
Palaces hover'd in the air!~
In thy laws written
Was only the death sentence!

The transgression of modesty
Is not thy fetter, nak'd expression of nudity
Thou wantest, knowest not aught of shame and
Diffidence! He who bow'd down his head
Thou hast held it high! Smilingly the dying people fasten
Ropes around their necks with thy hints, on
Thy bosom thou hast kindl'd the pit of indigence, with
Obnoxious pleasure thou hast brought them death!

Holding her crown thou bringest down
Laksmi to the ground!
Like *Sharada* striking on *vina's* strings
Which melody thou wantest to bring,
O the talent'd? But a scream only
I doth hear from the melody !

Waking up in the morn I hearken'd *kali's* song
Out there, the dismal cry of *sahnai* sadly drifts along!
As if someone return'd not home!
As if *sahnaiya* calls them home!
Hearts of loving wives are wafted
Away with the melody of *Sahnai* to their belov'd ~
Far, far away,
They're on their way!
The confidante says, 'Why dost thou not wipe tears,
Wipest thou kohl from thy eyes?'...
To this day waking up first in the morn I hear
The crying of *sahnai* – 'Come here, come here'!
Melancholy *shefalika* dropeth like smiles
Of a widow— full of refreshing fragrance!
Paralyzing the flowers with its kisses the butterfly dances

On its restless wings in intoxication, in flowery-boastfulness!
With pollens its wings are yellow'd,
With nectar its body is smear'd,

A lively life all around!
Unknowingly I singeth the welcoming song
Of joy! For no reason my eyes are fill'd with tears!
The bond of unity with the world someone binds!
The world cometh forward with hands
Smear'd with clay offereth palm-full of flowers as gifts!
As if she is my loving daughter youngest !–
Suddenly I get worri'd! Oh ! My baby! Thou wakest up and cryest
For not eating anything since yesterday, the cruel ascetic,
Always in my home thou cryest, hungry thou art!

O my baby, my dear baby, little milk I couldn't offer
Thee to drink! No right have I to rejoice anymore!
In my home the unbearable poverty always cries
By being my son, by being my wife!
Now who will play the flute?
A joyful smile of beauty where can I get?
The flower-juice– *Datura!* I drinketh that
Glass-full of eye-soothing extract!....

Till today I listen to *sahnai* that sings the arrival song,
As if it weeps – nothing is there, nothing!
(Sindhu-hindol)

A few words:
Poet embraced the penury of his life with extreme gratefulness while he was dealing with worldly disappointments, setbacks and

financial hardship. He remained largely optimistic and accepted his indigence quietly. He compared the poverty with the thorny crown of Jesus Christ. He was much obliged to poverty for giving him the courage of speaking out unhesitatingly though he suffered and felt the bitterness of indigence around him and his family.

The Poet wrote this poem on 9th October 1926(24th Ashwin 1333 BD). In 1926 Poet Kazi Nazrul settled in Krishnanagar, Kolkata and wrote poetry and songs for the downtrodden and weak classes of the society. This famous poem Poverty ('Daridro') was written during that time.

*Falguni

Confidante, spread no lotus-leaf on rock-bed,
On me throw no rose petals, bother me not!
Heart that is beset with crying, heart that churns,
Give him not, O confidante, give him not lotus garland
Smear'd with sandalwood~
'Tis tormenting, awful!

Tell me, how I tame my fire in heart!
The spring killers came with arrows stain'd with blood!
As if it strikes with deadly sting!
Flower-buds are burst open,
Flowers~ young, worn out and old!
Those estrang'd girls are half-kill'd —
As if salt is pour'd on their wounds!

For drinking wine I was in a drunken stupor!
Everybody distributes fragrance, spreads more
Lemon's smell! Subdu'd are *ashok* and coral, *rangan* is embarrass'd there!
Bedazzling *Polash* and *shimul*'s redness bloom'd all over!

My dear, from flowers honey
Drops, but with sting bee inflicts me!
New buds in mango trees
Are companion of bees!
Bees kiss the mango-buds --
Inside me my heart grumbles!
There all the confidantes gather
In the *ghats*, everyday they fill the pitchers,
When gestures are not express'd fully,

Their cheeks become more beaming seemingly!

Flowers I cannot stand any more long!
Mollika, chapa in the morn,
In the eve *beli* and *chameli*! Look, there blooms
Flowers like befuddl'd angels,
The city of trees doth shimmer, there
Sajna flowers dropeth on the street, seeing flowers
All around aristrocrat women forget their status and clans!
Arranging plate with betel leaves, sitting with friends
On rooftop with hand-fans in hand they fan their kins,
Feelings they exchange through eyes, in whisperings —
They fall on each other's lap with false annoyance
By god *kama*'s influence!
Today excepting me everyone gets
What he wants!

O dear, pungent and sweet smell of food, the wind
Brings, 'tis like- more the chest burning more appetite
It brings,'tis intoxicating like wine, there coos
The black fac'd inauspicious cuckoo !
With blazing coloration big dish-like moon
Emits light all over pleasant greens!
Branches of trees are overwhelm'd,
Flowers and fruits are in coloration, bracelets
Jingle! Spring festival goes all around!
But 'tis me who cries in seclusion!

So many aristrocrat women tear their saris
With thorns of jujube ! Confidante, my shores
Are full of flowers without thorns!
Bee stings on flowers?

My friend, better it would have been
If my shores were prick'd all over by thorns!
(Shindu-hindul)

A few words:

It was a spring season (March 1926, Falgun, 1332 BD) when Poet wrote this poem. He was in Hugli, India at that time.

* The word Falguni is related to the word Falgun. The word Falguni refers to the characteristics and the salient features of the Falgun, the 11th month of the Bangla calendar year. It is the month of the spring season in Bangladesh when colorful flowers bloom all around in all flowering plants. The Poet sees and feels the charm and beauty of the spring month Falgun through a girl who describes her feelings to her confidante that she perceived from the colorations all around her in the nature.

Welcoming A Bride

For so long a time to this world thou didst belong,
Today thou belongest to a home of thy own,
On the dust of the earth thou comest down
Today, in the dream, in poet's imagination
Thou hadst been a half bloom'd lotus,
Graceful for so many days!
At the setting twilight hour today thou hadst
Set thy foot on a mind-captivating beach!
The *sindur* of the dawn by the wind
Was blown away from the *sithi* of thy head!

The princess of dawn becomes a charming wife in the evening,
Moon's spotless face is mark'd with spots of *chandan* !
The fidgety, restless wants to put the veil
Today o'er her head amid bashful
Happiness, with passionate outburst
The she-pigeon warbles, a fairy-tale thou wert,
Today a graceful wife thou art!

Restless and swinging
This home was with thy braid's frequent flappings,
The amass'd happiness
Dazzles in the gems of thy necklace!
Happiness of the home thou takest in thine eyes,
Kindlest the lamp with that light, let the tears
Remain in the eyes today —
In this conduit of union let the smile and gay
Of home, the *behag raga* of flute cry
In the tone of *sahnai*!

Every one today in wedding coloration,
Color'd mind, color'd outfits, O the woman,
Say- 'Today is my day of new awakening'.
Be a charioteer of thy husband
Not in sin, but in virtuous devotion.
If he's blind, O the chaste,
Do not blind-fold him, rather let thy honest
Behavior be the sight
To thy husband blind!
[Shindu-Hindol]

A few words:
When poet's lover entered into someone's life as a new bride, he recalled vividly many memories that lasted in his mind. In one line of the poem he advised her to be a charioteer of her husband's life and to reckon the day of 'welcoming a bride' as a day of new awakening.

The Bond Of Friendship

[Rakhibandhan]
The charming earth and sky today make friendship with autumn?
From the blue sky with gifts the boat of clouds comes down!
The cloud's pleasing harbinger- the geese
Fly towards the land of riches with colorful *Kalmi*-buds!
Embroider'd with *Seunti*-design the confidante wears
The turquoise *Peshwaj*,
In a path across the open field with each other the skyey
And earthly confidantes make a fellowship!

Foggy scarf, bluish corset
The sky brought forth,
Tips of stars, garland of thunder and
A necklace of two-day old crescent moon!
An orchestra play'd in the sky in rattling sound
Of downpour, in shrieking calls of *papiya*
And *shayma* –
Between the two
A friendship grew!

Wind, the slave of the sky
Brings white cumulus clouds—foamy and flowery,
Here in the water, in the land,
In the lotus white and red!
The unkempt earth becomes jittery!
O what a deluge in the sky,
The monsoon sings the songs with mode,

Delight'd cloud-maidens pull the rope of boat!

The boatmen worri'dly stare
At the clouds, on them the cloud-girls spray
Water and say:
'Look at us, ye wicked guys'!

The sky tells the earth, 'O the confidante, at night send
Thy *Chokor*, for him I'll snatch a moon!
Moon-lit ambrosia thy son
Can drink as much as he can
To content his thirst! In exchange send
Me thy earthly smell, sweetness
Of the morning-flower, fragrance
Of thy soil, the *raga Purobi* of the evening!'

The luminous sky laugh'd, with thrill it bents down;
With herbs, creepers and flowers earth entwin'd
With the sky and said: 'Confidante,
Today with the earth thou art tied',
The sky embrac'd the earth, shiver'd
In shyness it bent down and kiss'd the earth!
[Shindu-Hindol]

A few words:
Rakhibandan is a tradition in Hindu society where one ties a colorful thread around someone's wrist in the month of Shravana – the fourth month of Bangla calendar year—which symbolizes the bond of friendship. The Poet in the poem describes the friendship and love between the sky and the earth and their interaction with other natural bodies like clouds, rain, moon, trees, flowers and

the birds- all are in a bond of friendship in the nature. The poet might have directed the theme of the poem-' a bond of friendship' towards us so that 'the human being' should conceive it and love each other making a bond of friendship.

In a Moon-lit Night

In the horizon's blue river an extravaganza is emanat'd
From the multicolor'd floating clouds!
Struggling there the star-bubbles in the multi-color'd
Moon-lit night! Aboard a 'shampan' of the three-day old
Moon the sky-darling moves ahead,
Anxious is the sky-sea with her little doll
In the bosom! Around the three-day old moon perceptible
Is a round indistinct line, cover'd
Up in a veil- the blue 'gul rukh'- the belov'd
Of the azure horizon, the sky-queen sleeps on
The star-bed of the Ursa Major! A misty mosquito-curtain
Laili has rigg'd up, she appear'd silently there, in horizon
The densely shadow'd green belt of trees,
The misty mosquito-curtain made of fog is on the edge?
With a bouquet of twenty-seven stars the sky
Came down in deep night, nearby
His belov'd in the bed of stars he slept silently,
From her sleep the blue angel woke up annoyingly,
Seeing that from a hidden place the papiya coo'd,
Kindling the lamp of benefaction the star Mongal stay'd
Awake, the flame of lamp flickers by his lover's breath!
The kalpurusha, the sky's door keeper strolls, passes
Sleepless night holding a search-light of burning meteors.
In the garden the confidantes gather'd secretly, to
And fro they run and laugh with the tone of cuckoo!
In passion, in love, sweat drops from the chin
Of the sky-queen like dew on a moon-saucer! O the confidante!
Who's that moon-lit Shiraji pouring wine
To his wife's lip? Saying—'Drink Tahura , O my darling'!

Thinking of someone the indolent lonely saki from afar
Makes sketches on moon-saucer in the gathering of stars!
Farhad-Shiri-Laili- Majnu are cracking their brain,
In the violin of wind the rowdy shayma and dadhial play the tone!

O the unmindful Saki! In this way unknowingly the scandalous-flower
You oft draw and erase from the cup of my heart's corner!

The Solace

O there bloom'd the mind-bud *Hasnahena* in the darkness
   of death!
Surpassing the life's barricade the fragrance of her bosom
   had spread!
Breaking the wall of the prison escap'd all prisoners,
Hence in the crematorium gather'd all the anxious hearts
Of the universe! O the earth is illuminat'd there
By the light of ruinous flame of fire!

The lotus-heart of the *Swaraj* party tumbl'd at the feet
Of the king of the universe! The white beam of lotus shin'd
The party's mind, the handsome prince swings
In the *ShishMohal*,
The incomparable!
To the dead *Bashudeva* there goes
The captive *Keshob*!
In the future *Brindaban*
The mother *Jashuda* blows the conch!

The one who is asleep tonight will wake up tomorrow
   morning.
In the rising dawn darkness of farewell will be shining!
To every home the dew of the sad night will bring crops,
Again empty branches of winter will be blossom'd with
   flowers.
In the night the mother who lull'd the baby into sleep,
Will wake him up in the morning again with a kiss!

If cold dew of the dead-night would not drop in the life's
   sea,

There would be no pearls of freedom, the life-oyster would die.
In the pearl of the world-eye no jewel of tears would shine!
The ambrosia of the moon would not melt down
If the furnace of the sun would not have extinguish'd.
At the horizon the evening lamp of the sky would not be kindl'd.

Today let not the axe sever the old bamboo flute,
Right here, in this flute the melody of *Braja's* flute will be play'd!
In this ceremony of union the flutist will be around
This time, besmear'd with the ash of cremation
The *Shiva* will play that horn-bugle of creation!
In this enormous pain of the world Jesus will be born again.

If there is no rest in the work, there would be no peace!
The crops will grow— otherwise
The world-eye would not shed tears!
For its outer part no affinity a seed bears,
That's why shadow of the trees it brings,
If 'twas not born, it would not have been
Laugh'd at the time of death! It will come again— otherwise
The earth wouldn't have lov'd it so much!
[Chittonama]

A few words:
It is the poet's only solace that one day in the darkness of death the fragrance of night flowers will spread around, pearls of freedom will not allow the oysters to die, in the twilight-horizon a lamp of hope and happiness will be kindled, the earth will be illuminated by the light of ruinous flame of fire.

When The Indra Descends

The sun is yet to be set, all on a sudden
In the sky the rumbling of drums has begun!
Which arrival song for *Indra* all over the sky is being sung?
The roaring of an elephant I hear in the massive sound
Of the conch of clouds!
Hair-raising neighing of thunderbolts
Emanates from the stable of clouds,
On its first day the *Ashar* has
Shown its cataclysmic face!

At the north-eastern corner of the horizon
The fog accumulates, overwhelm'd with pain
The horizon-girls listen to a terrible crying!
Plants and creepers, birds and beasts start'd wailing,
Smear'd with earth's sacred dust the Indra ascends the heaven!
Joyful drum-beats are all over in the horizon,
There in the sky the lightning-girls dance in amusement!
The Indra of earth sits beside the Indra of heaven,
With seven notes the seven
Skies generate grave clapping sound,
In the earth echoes that sound —
Empty, all o'er the emptiness!

Alas ! O the helpless all-enduring reticent mother
Earth, shall I only make my offering to thee with flowers
That lost lustre? Thine hungry son will remain ever discontent'd?-
Ambrosia couldn't fill thine earthen pot?
Churning the sea of life if someone

Brings the ambrosia, god's rage will fall upon
His head? It may or may not be, but I know it truly
The heaven needs whom the earth loves really!

In the lotus of thorns bloom'd the mind-lotus,
Graceful it became in the blood-red-foot of *bani*,the goddess!
Humbly bent down the worshipper and tore apart
That lotus as his best offering in oblation at the feet
Of *Narayan*! We know, we know, he who carries the conch,
Wheel and rod, eternal will be the lotus in his hand!
So much faith, solace and hope like mirage
Appear in the sahara of sorrows,
But that satiat'd
Not the thirsty heart!

With the jewelless-hood the snake king dangles, dangles the earth,
Today which star will be illuminate its hood!
The charming earth I beheld waking up in the morn,
In the name of god the satan recites the opening song,
O the rebel, the saint, the ascetic, the great man!
With thine gesture, I saw all on sudden the creation
Stopp'd, the moon, the sun and stars paus'd
Momentarily, its rule the cruel fate forgot
And the destiny respond'd!

Whene'er a mistake the creator made, thou hast
Reform'd it, the creator salut'd thee before thou didst!
Whene'er an unconscious *Narayan* thou hast seen,
By a kick his consciousness thou hast brought in
As did the *Bhrigu*, the world trembl'd in fear! With thine

Foot-print on his chest, the Indian
God of destiny tells everyone—
'In this way the truth I acknowledge!'
To stir up the truth the one who has
So much right, anxiousness—
My million salutations to his truth-awareness!

Thine graceful chronicle
Of creation today I recall,
With thine sweet voice thou didst
Appear in *Bani's* lotus forest!
When with golden lotus-petals thy vina was cover'd,
Suddenly I saw the sacrificial sun was on thine forehead!
Lakshmi offer'd thee golden petals -
Bani offer'd vina, on thy body Shiva smear'd sacrificial
Ashes, Vishnu gave thee the dumbel of destruction,
Flute is offer'd by *Jashudha's* son,
Heat is offer'd by the sun,
A smile by the moon!

The mother India bless'd thee with perpetual dust of gold -
Shibaji initiat'd thee with vedic hymn and
Bound a turban on thy head!
The Buddha gave alms-pots,
Nimai gave his bags,
All the gods offer'd thee a *mandar*-garland,
With dust anoint'd thou art by mankind!
Thou art the universal arouser of pleasing mind,
From across the universe thou hast risen —
The great hero, the poet, the rebel, the giver,
The lover, the wise and the worker!
All the obstacles wash'd away

From the mighty Himalaya,
From the vast open sky like grasses of bower
By the stream of thine life! There
Thou art beyond the rhythm of song, O the saint!
That's why in my whole life thee I ador'd not,
The ashes of the pyre of my heart I brought!
O the great power, anoint'd with sandal-paste
From *Kailash* thou returnest!
O the poet of the crematorium, the offerings
Of the burnt ashes I brought! Take my offerings,
Take my palm-full of offerings,
Today the songs of my untold tale I brought
With bitterness of anguish! Thou hadst
Lov'd me so much, no time hadst thou
Given me to love thee, that's why cries my heart today!

Whate'er pain I've in this world of pain and sorrows,
In my heart I look for solace, yet in grief my heart cries!
Today is the fall of Indra of India, a difficult time for the world!
The lifeless Bengal is shock'd, bewilder'd !
In grief the heart growls off and on, my tears
Have taken my words!
Thou art the friend of the poor, friend
Of the country and mankind,
Look around, the world tumbles to kiss thy feet!
At the horizon the crowds have gather'd,
The rain began to pour as usual!
Getting wet in the rain fall
Thine many memories are
Getting heavier –

Born we are not in the era of prophets and incarnations!
We saw not them, nor did we see their astral formation,
Whene'er had I any chance to sit near thy feet,
Knowing not anything, not
Discerning anything –tearful were my eyes!
As if my heart by being a palm-full of offerings
Tumbl'd down at thy feet!
Bloom'd is my pride into a prostration sweet!
Buddha made a great sacrifice,
I saw him not with my eyes.
O'er it I lament not!
Nimai became an ascetic-mendicant,
But him I offer'd not any rich gift,
The lord of love we have seen, the king-mendicant!

We heard, a saint sacrific'd his life offering his skeletons!
O *Harishchandra* of the new age, respond!
In a crematorium holding her
Baby in the lap the bewailing chaste mother wanders
To and fro, look back O the king of saints!
Abandoning the kingdom, wife and son thou hadst
Taken control of India-crematorium alone
In disguise of *chandal*,
O the ascetic, O the emperor, come
Today to this crematorium,
Listen to the cry
Of thine virtuous 'life' baby!

Like *Datakarna* thou hast put thy son's head
On the stake and cut him into pieces with a sword!
Like Abraham, in the name of truth thou wert
About to sacrifice thy son with the knife, O thou, the heart

Of a Prophet!
All angels salute
Thee! To thee all deities bow down,
Awaits most spendid seat for a godly man!

The king Rama, the belov'd, abandon'd
His wife *Shita*, Rama need'd *Janoki* 's help in his burnt-
Offerings, thy own treasure-house, the *Laksmi*,
Thou hast hand'd o'er to the hungry and thirsty,
The dust of road thou hast scoop'd up for thyself,
In thine own burnt-offerings of life help
Of *Hem* and *Laksmi* thou dost need, burnt thou wert
In the sacrificial fire, but what thou hadst
Abandon'd, taken not back! Like *Biswamitra* through meditation
Power thou hast earn'd, to thee all the Brahmins
Of the world bow down!

O the *Vishma* of the ages! Lying on the death-bed
Of despise thou hast left the heroic words for the world!
In thine life-time thou hast told us— the *panchajanya* of eternal
Truth and the great geeta of Krishna will fall
Down on the injurious *Kuruksetra* before the arrival
Of Vishnu in his last incarnation,
The pyre of oppression burns
With fat-burnt smoke through ages!
Thou art the new sage,
Thou didst write down new life, the new age of India —
Thou hast shown the *Shachi*—the garland of *parijat* is for *Indra* !
Shattering the pillars of the palace of tyrants all on a sudden

Thou hast appear'd as an incarnation
Of *Nri-shinha* of the new age, the *Prahlada* with his heart
Of humanity for the oppressors jump'd
Into thy bosom with tremendous devotion
For the freedom of love! Thou, the life-ganges, streamest down!
The gods are overwhelm'd watching *Nimai* embrac'd thee,
On his lap the Buddha put thee!

Suspicion arous'd in nobody's mind whether thou art
Hindu or Muslim or somebody else! Thou art
For the distress'd, thou art for the pain,
Thou art for all --the way the sun
Distributes light, the flower distributes pleasure!
Thou art *Aurongazeb* to Muslim, to Hindu *Akbar*!
Where'er the pain of life thou hast perceiv'd, there
Shiva thou hast seen! Taking the blame of slender
And despise on thy shoulder, O the mad, thou hast
Bridg'd the heart of Hindu-Muslim! I know not what
Oblation should be offer'd by the Hindu and Muslim to-
     day to thee,
Let their life be bloom'd as a lotus in the mud of jealousy!
O the conqueror of enemies, victorious thou art, O the lover,
Today thine crematorium is full of friends and brothers!
So I see, those who gave thee thorns and stings,
They brought today offerings of flowers,
Who thou art, no one knows, a deity or a saint !
Only I know ~ seeing none but thee my heart is full of
     content!

Today everywhere the people of revolution
Look for the dwellings! Around
The Nag-babies thou wert the fence of cactus!

Thou hast pick'd up Vishnu's lotus
From the foot of king's elephant
And hand'd it over again to Vishnu's hand!
The flute thou hast seen at the gopi's gallows,
Brindaban of love thou hast creat'd on the bank of sorrows
Of bloody *Jamuna* ! With its broken wheels they drove thy chariot,
They shin'd their way with illuminating jewesl of their heads!
The shelterless lost their way,
Wayfarers they are today,
Sitting at the cave-entrance in a fatal tone
The snake charmer plays his flute!

Where'er I look! Only frustration, any shore I see not!
Who is that curs'd self-ruler grabb'd the wheel of chariot?
In the battle *Judhistir* faught with *Sabbyashachi*,
Look there, the *Kaurava* soldiers dancing in ecstasy!
With utter noise the fire arrow pierces the Himalaya it finds,
The crying-Ganges is lagging behind!
Out of fear the bewilder'd Himalaya hides itself in the clouds!
The world-sea of tears might want it to be drown'd !
Pride he lost, with shame his high head is down'd,
The Himalaya has risen from prostration!
From the matt'd hair of Dhurjuti the Ganges weeps and flows,
The pyre burns, as if on Shiva's fore-head it glows!

Eternal was the death by the touch of thy life!
Its black face was full of light,

In the crematorium songs were sung! Sweet fragrance
All around from the burning sandalwood and flowers –
Fire became sacred, deads were the graceful!
Besmear'd with thine pyre-ashes, the tributary of *Bhagiroti* was thankful!
Thy touch made the fire-wood pure and clean,
At an untimely inauguration
Of the *Ashur*-killer Rama went there
To pluck out her eyes that I remember;
From thy life palm-full of flowers thou hast offer'd! O the king saint!
The India is longing to see when '*Dhonuja-duloni*' will rise again!
[Chittanama]

A few words:

Poet portrayed himself here in this poem as Indra of earth who was a rebel, a saint, an ascetic and a great man! As Indra the Poet constantly waged war against the oppressors who opposed morality, equality and humanity. He descended to the land of India with his chariot to carry the people of India. He was the Indra for both Muslims and Hindus of India. He saw the same pain of subjugation, distress and sorrows in both Hindus and Muslims. He took the slander and blames on his own shoulder and longed for that day when India will rise.

Indra: In Vedic myth of Hinduism, Indra is described as the king of the gods. He has authority over the sky and the power to make rain using his weapon the thunderbolt.

He is the king of the gods. He is warrior, protector and reformer.

The King-Beggar

Which tone of the flute of a homeless vagrant
Woke thee up! O the e'er-phlegmatic?
Leaving thine golden-lotus-garden thou hast
Stood up on the dust,
O the e'er-phlegmatic?

O the loving son of the King, thou wert
In drowsiness, thou knowest not
A hungry destitute wanders on the roads
Begging for food to eat,
The god of ambrosia woke up and cri'd–
'Hungry', 'I'm hungry', O the e'er-phlegmatic?!

Colorful thou hast made thy body with red ochre of pain,
Amid shivering and startling the illusionary sleeping
City woke up from sleep! In the morning
Their King the city-people beheld without food
Begging from door to door, mingl'd
Was thine golden body with dust
Of roads, the *Narayan* thou art!
To share the pain of the world
In a new form thou hast appear'd!
O the e'er-phlegmatic?

Thou sayest, 'Give me alms', the king beggar
Stands at the door,
No alms thou hast receiv'd, no one open'd the door;
Fearful thou art for the doorman standing at the door!
Sayest thou, 'Will you not give me alms?
Take this gift from me –'tis my life, full of alms'!

No alms they offer'd thee,
They took no gift, thou art the *Yogi*
Turn'd back to walk!
That life nobody could take, was taken by the death!
(Chittanama)

The Gift Of Autumn

The season's dish filled
With gifts of the earth had arriv'd!
With the smell of newly husk'd
Paddy, today the autumn is subdu'd!
Plate-full of *firnee* of 'Gini-pagal' rice
The newly marri'd wife offers
Her husband with smiles,
Amid happiness her hand shivers!
The older wife cooks *shirnee*, the house is full
Of smell!

Today delight'd are both husband and wife,
Their farm is full of paddy. In low voice the younger wife
Sings the song while preparing her bed!
The mother-in-law regrets—
'The *mejla* son-in-law visit not us
Long since!' Her younger daughter says—
'Mother, *Mejo* sister weeps
Everyday!' *Shejo* wife feels
Like dying to arrange betel nuts
And leaves for the portico guests!

Today the neighborhood naughty boys all
Make hue and cry! Clad in *moinamoti sari* the girls dazzle
With ornaments! Wearing new armlets
The boastful farmer's wife talk less now-a- days,
With *Jari* and *shari* songs lively is the village!
Mouth gets watery when the wives
Make *pita* with lot of sweet! In the sea of crop field
The low tide begins after the high tide!

In the flute of a shepherd
The farewell tone was play'd
In the field of winter paddy,
The farmer sings *bhatiyali*,
So bereav'd, bemoaning is the parting-melody!
While farmer's wife husks the paddy
A wave of beauty ripples over her body!
Her lively foot brings life to the wooden *dheki* !

O, leaning back on the autumn the winter basks in the sun!
With its beam the sun tumbles down –
The stream of light! In the horizon there
As if a Turkish virgin appears
Taking off her misty-veil! The night awakes
Alone by kindling a moon-lamp. The green leaves
Turn'd into yellowish while awaiting
A change for the new coming!

There come the leaves tender
Hoisting red flag of new comers!
Flags they are not of blood, but of victorious
Branches! The autumn brings good news—
Here comes the new year's day,
Open the gate, fill up the store house of paddy
With the smile saved from the whole year!
There wakes up a lovely baby without fear
In the morning in his us'd
Old bed!
[Jinjhir]

A few words:

The Poet portrayed a picture of joyful life of village farmers who just harvested paddy in the autumn months of the year. He described also the vibrant happiness that equally spread in the mind of the house-wives of the happy village farmers.

*Mrs. M. Rahman

The moon of *Moharram* is yet to be risen!
Which mournful wailing of *karabala* then
I hear around me! Why the waves
Of Euphrates began whimpering in my eyes!
Crowd'd there all the crying orphans
In my mind-eyes! Morshia-khan! Sing not the mourning song!
Over-flow'd will be the earth by the deluge of tears
Of all-sacrificing people there !.....

On my way to *Kufa* in the *Karbala* I stopp'd,
Around me all the *Yazid*-soldiers I behold!
On their palms with the enemy-blood
My brothers smear hena, pain inflict'd I lie at the sick-bed!
Without food and water I'm on the bed of grass lying motionless !
All on a sudden appear'd there '*Duldul*' saddleless,
Someone cries out, '*Zainul Abedin* !' Leaving the thatch'd hut
With sickly body in haste I came out,
The doorman stopp'd me there!
From the bank of the life-*Furat* I listen there
To the call of my imprison'd mother!
The barrier of *Yazid* I trespass'd, cried out
The caravan in the middle of night!
The *Yazid* is after me, how can I trace *Azrael* ?
By the sands of sahara my life is all
Surround'd! Fire of sea I drink making the hell
Empty ! With the pain I burn, water dries up in the eyes,
With chest breaking growling my heart pulpits!

Remember! Cri'd *Hassan, Hussain*
For their deceas'd mother Fathima in pain!

To keep afloat frantically I struggle near
The shore of pain in the deluge of tears,
My own loss seriously I accept while forgetting other's
Loss, I forget~ so many baby-birds
Beneath the cool shadow of baniyan tree took shelter
Like me being forgetful of their own mothers !
Motherly comfort so many pain-afflict'd travelers
Receiv'd while sitting underneath the tree! All fatigueness
They forgot! They bemoan amidst my words,
The pain in me becomes the pain of the world !
Gather'd around me the unfathomable tears of many eyes!
In the middle I'm, the pain-lotus, on the verge
Of tumbling ! kind was mother for the whole
World !While foreshaking others no right I have to cry
    alone!

Being an elder brother I came to your grave, mother,
Along with motherless younger brothers and sisters !
For shedding tears my eyes turn'd blind yet
They thought I might know the trace that
You gave me, O mother ! Being insolvent
In the dawn of life those who walk'd
Towards graveyard
With meaningless songs,
You shelter'd them with deep affection,
Spreading your wings around them,–there
They Embrace each other
All the home-abandon'd,
In your lap, in your home shelter they found!

You us'd to say, 'Since the sky is open,
Millions of stars, moon, sun it can
Accommodate, that space not fill'd up yet, space
Still there--only emptiness can fill up that emptiness!

We, the grave-absconders, understand
That not, O mother that debt of graveyard
You paid by being a surety yourself! The homeless
You console with the key of your own home with less
Stress, thus our debt you paid up by the death! Such
A service you render'd to all, in return you took not
Anybody's service! The light spreads light
To everybody, who gives light to the light?
Cry more deeply the pain inflict'd words than we do!
There stops the crying of her loving daughter too!
Cyclone rumbles no more in the lotus garden,
In the prison the drum-beats make no more breaking sound!
When the Muslim of Bengal will sit
On the throne of knowledge! Not
To write the word 'mim' the pen
Drops from your hand again and again!

A lost Arab beduin-daughter she was! Us'd
To cry while looking at the high wall of the harem! Want'd
To breathe the same light and air like others!
Fail'd to leap over the bondage-barrier,
She leap'd over her life! Said she, "That *Harem* is not
For those women who forgot
The slavery by the charm of harem! Keeping
The slave-women in suspicion

Men's beastly desire become prominent !
The sacrificing women had surrender'd
To the greedy desire of prison-police ! Mention'd
Nowhere in Qur'an,
Hadith or in history of Islam that women
Are the slave of men,
In harem years together women
Were prison'd!Those who trade with Qur'an,
Hadith and fikah, obey they not the message of Qur'an –
"Men and women are equal"! Something convenient
They pick up for themselves from the scriptures,
About women remain they silent ~ thieves they are!
Hypocrites she detect'd who steal in broad day light !
Their hands with knife she gripp'd,
In mosque they inflict Islam with that
Knife! This expedition you made to bring the light
In the hearts of women-slaves, frighten'd they are
By the harem-guards! Each other
They rebuke, exchange no bullets!
Understand they not, if someone spits
On the sky, on his face it drops ! Abusing words they hurl'd
On you, those words bloom'd into flowers- at your feet they dropp'd!

the Nag mother you were With upright hood
In the garden of cactus, they came to hit you, instead
They hit on your devotion!
In your poisonous zone of galaxy new stars were born
To arouse rebellion in the prohibit'd world, O Mother,
Drinking poison your snake-babies have built the banner
Of triumph! The fetter of all rules and regulations
They ignor'd, ignor'd all obstructions and prohibitions,

For the stray'd cattle the enclosures
were not built for the man but for cows and sheeps!

Like an amulet your soul is clean
And holly containing words divine,
Surround'd they're by the reticent pain?
Or in the garden of Fathima, the 'Khatun-e Jannath',
Prick'd with rose-thorns there
Bloom'd flowers
In blood red color?

High tide those who creat'd in your sea of pain,
Where are they now? Where the moon
Dies when dri'd up is the sea?

For those you sacrific'd untimely your life, let again
Your sacrifice be meaningful through the uprising!
In the mid way, mother, that flame of light
Of your life was extinguish'd, let it
Be blaz'd again as a mark of victory on
The parting of hair of the women
Of the world, Mother, alive you're in the pain
Of the women-prisoners, to kiss the dust again
Your grave I visit! On the path
Of life you walk'd towards the death,
Do you walk today towards life
Leaping o'er the death?
[Jinjhir]

A few words:
This poem was about a lady(Mrs. M Rahman) whom he respected like a mother. She was his source of inspiration to write many

poems on struggling women and their rights. Her untimely death shrouded him with immense grief. He wrote this poem as a gesture of respect and recognition to her contribution she made during her short life. Her death would be meaningful only through the uprising of the suffering women of world that poet had felt deeply.

Poet wrote- her soul was clean like an amulet and sacred that contained divine words. In the sea of pain like a moon she created a high tide.

Mrs. M Rahman was also known as Mrs. Masuda Khatun(1885-1926), one of the pioneering women in Bengal (India) who faught for the women's rights and equality in the conservative society of both elites and common people of Bengal. She was a writer, columnist and an activist. She was a secularist and committed to Hindu-Muslim unity. She organized a center for rehabilitating prostitutes in Calcutta (Kolkata).

Poet Kazi Nazrul Islam praised her work and commitment. He addressed her always as 'mother' and considered her as a source of inspiration.

Eid Mubarok

Passing through so many deserts,
Traversing so many miles, shedding so much tears
On desert's sand there comes the *Eid* after many years!
Carrying the gifts of pleasure at the doors of beggars,
Bringing the hope of flowery garden
In the garden of thorns,
With content'd heart for more
Wine thou askest saki there!

The happy *papiya* chirps all around,
Sleeplessly the new bride spends the night!
Where's the flower vase! The flowers weep
There, someone passes nights without sleep
For his belov'd in a land far-off,
The typical smell he finds in the dishevel'd
Hair of his eager sweetheart,

O dear, what good news the moon could bring last night!
The tender minds seethe in delight,
From *sahnai* comes
Out the *ashabori raga*, with the fragrance
Of *atar* the cruel hearts are subdu'd!
People think not today their debt
In mortgage,
The documents for lease!

Today each other they embrace, the *Yazid* and *Hasan-Hussain*!
Friendly are the flowers of hell and heaven,
Shiri and *Farhad* cuddle each other, *Laili* twists around *Qais*
Like a snake! In pleasure wife closes her eyes

In her husband's embrace!

Today with flames the joy of hell burns,
Where some satans poured down wine!
In congregation stand the enemy and friend,
Every village is the valley of *Arafat* and
Like brothers the king and beggar
Embrace each other,
But *lat-manat-* the two deities
Dance around in Kaba-premises!

Spreads all o'er today the sound of Islamic drum,
No status- higher and lower-equal are all human beings
No one is no one's king or subject!
Who's that *Ameer*? Art thou a *Nawab* or a king, livest
In a multi-stori'd mansion?
Through ages thou art a person disgrac'd;
Ah! In real Islam confusion thou hast creat'd!

Islam says, we're all for each other,
Happiness and sorrows equally we share,
No right we have to hoard money! Someone's chandeliers
Would be kindl'd by the tears of others?
A few will be fortunate
And million others will be unfortunate?
The rule of Islam 'tis not!

Hence the *Eidul-Fitr* reminds
Us the reign of Islam again,
O thou who made some savings, spend thy
Surplus for others as charity,
Let thy food be the food for the hungry!

In thy hand overflows the cup of pleasure
Whereon the thirsty one have a share,
Enjoy the pleasure by sharing it,
O the big heart'd!

With clean heart today pay the *zakat*,
O the spend-conscious, do not do math
Today on thy spending! Make an error
Today in counting thy figures!
Desperate are the lovers for love,
Today Shaila-Laila kiss the Yogi!
In exchange
Of jewel they want wine!

Each other we greet today on the streets,
Saying *Eid Mubarok! As salam!* O my friends,
Today *shirnee* will be fed,
The holy revelation will be spread!
O today with my love of charity the *Eidgah* glows!
While offering charity to everyone's
Hand, 'tis the heart, not
The body gets the reward
As the one who is martyr'd![Jinjhir]

A few words:

He described the joyous day of Eid celebration, a festival of Muslim. In the poem he brought forward the significance of the Eid day--worshiping the God of the Universe in congregation prayer showing the equality of status, rank and colors in Islam with utmost sincerity and open heart and offering some amount of money, charity and food to the indigent.

Who Wants To Go To Heaven

Come who wants to go to heaven—
The most exalted door of life, the song
Of alive and dead they sing in the perpetual
Gathering of the youths eternal!
Come who wants to go to heaven!

With youths the place is crowded,
Can go there no saint old,
Those who search for scriptures
Like vultures,
Work hard for gaining knowledge,
To the garden of angels and *sakis*
No admittance they can gain!
Come who wants to go to heaven!

Prevails there always a spree of enjoyment,
Around you is a flock of charming attendants
Ready for service, here always
Heart wants *dil-afruz,*
Heart is tied with *piran,*
Come who wants to go to heaven!

Those who made no mistake in life, trampl'd
No thorn under the feet, pluck'd
No flowers, protect'd only the fence of garden
As a gardener and cared for that Eden,
Unwanted they're here
At the angel's soiree!
Come who wants to go to heaven!

Alas! Spending whole life in water the old man of principle
Got not a drop of water from the pebbles!
His fingers are bruis'd by the thorns,
From his neck hangs the flowers' garland!
Come, who wants to go to heaven!

Considered they're not as righteous,
Slowly they kill themselves along with others,
At the door they lie down
On the day of *Eid* in starvation,
Come, who wants to go to heaven!

The nightingale whispers to everyone—
They threaten'd the garden,
Obstract'd the blooming flowers to bloom,
Under the feet they trampl'd them
Lest sweet smell they spread,
Guests unwant'd
They're in a poetry-reading gathering!
Come, who wants to go to heaven!

Here a young man sings intoxicating *gazal*
With *dilruba* at his lap, a charming mole
He puts on the unspott'd
Cheek of his sweet heart
In an exotic dance!
Come, who wants to go to heaven!

Here 'no entrance' for the unreligious, lifeless,
Decrepit! No difference in blood and wine in this
Assembly of youths, with flowers' garland
The bow is tied!

Come, who wants to go to heaven!

Here the cups contain blood of martyr,
Sword-sharp fresh youths are there,
O hearts are dipp'd in the glasses of wine
Color'd like glowing sun!
Here lovers and martyrs remain vigilant!
Come, who wants to go to heaven!

O the moon I see in the face of my lover,
And the lover's face in the moon! I make sin here
Willfully, willfully I build an embankment of sand
On the sandy beach of sea of enjoyment!
Come, who wants to go to heaven!
[Jinjhir]

A few words:
In the poem the poet narrated satirically that everyone can go to heaven but not without the wisdom of virtue. While doing the sinful deeds no one can enjoy the heavenly bliss and the felicities therein.

The Persian New Year's Day

[Noroj]
The beauty who wants to trade today,
Come, come here in this fair of New year's day!
Today in this gathering of pretty faces,
Prevails there only the widespread restlessness!
The beauty is loot'd and utterly ravag'd!
Shaking off the shame and status
The graceful women offer their beauty with smiles
And glances for no price, just out of whims!
In this fair of New year's day!

The Prince, the Minister, and Nawab's son–
Are the buyers of this fair! the young
Jeweler looks for jewelry shops,
Desperately jewels he buys,
Just on pretence the Prince of beauty of this *Noroj*
Touches Jahanara's robe!

The Princess and
The Queen roam around,
Their pretty faces are without veil?
What the sale-girls sell
In the empty shops no one knows!
The tingling sounds of conch bangles,
The tender *kori* and *rekab*, unrestrain'd,
Bargaining extravagant!
Golden cheeks
And red roses!

With *derhem* the slave-girls beg for hearts
In this new gathering of *noroj*!
The king, the slave, the killer, the lover
The queen, the slave-girl today equal they are!
Glances they exchange from eyes to eyes,
With each other they talk in their hearts!
Desperate they're, from garden they distribute flowers!
In the new gathering of *noroj*!

With sweet *sherbet* lips are drench'd,
Tingling of *nupur* in the feet!
Today talks are brief
In the resin like lips!
Today someone's *chadar* drops on someone's feet,
Someone's arm is around someone's waist,
Today in delirium the mind-peacock expands
Its feathers, in mind no patience!

Boundless love the balance of eyes weighs,
Whose necklace of tears weigh much
They balance! Today no cost for transaction!
At the end of transaction price drops down not on
Anything 'extra'! In exchange of betel-leaves,
Munna begs for the necklace of jewels!
Heart is restless!

Hearts they want to ruin today deliverately,
Someone is half-kill'd, someone is kill'd completely!
The thin waist dazzles, frenziedly shudders the *peswaz*,
The body's overburden'd with overweigh'd thighs,
Tears on the verge of dropping down! *Hafez, Omar, Shiraj*
Are wrting '*rubai*', hiding themselves away from the crowds!

Someone is half-kill'd,
Someone is completely slaughter'd,

Shiri looks for *Laili*, *Farhad* looks for *Qais*
In this land of Noroj!
The young *Shelim* looks for *Nurjahan*,
The languid *Aurogazeb* is in relaxation!
The diamond '*koohinur*' is nobody's desire
In the the land of Noroj here!

This moonlit land belongs to angel '*Gul bakauli*',
Here you just want the beauty only !
Let everything be drown'd here~
In the wine and *Saki*, in beauty and color,
In the smoke of *dhup*, in fragrance of *atar*,
Let all eyes become unwinking!
Here you draw the black moles on the faces pretty!
Just you want here only the beauty !

Indolent is everybody in frenzi'd enjoyment,
In *rangmohal* and in wine red!
In this fair of pretty faces of Noroj
Open up all the shops of *Momtaj*,
There comes the lover of beauty- *Shahjahan*
Again to shop around!
A far-distant picture of the future *Tajmohal*
The Poet has envision'd,~ the dream of *Noroj*!
[Jinjhir]

My words:
In Persian New Year's Day joyful alluring women gathered where

life was vibrant all over the place. The poet put forward the theme of the poem in the last lines of the poem where he envisioned the future India (Tajmohal) as a land of happiness – that day poet's true dream of noroj will be fulfilled.

The Front-travelers

March ahead with strong steps! O the soldiers,
The front-travelers!
Listen! O my sun-burnt dust-smear'd brothers,
In this deprav'd earth you're the first expeditioner,
Keep the weapons ready in armory, O the soldiers,
At night throw the fire-arrows!
Where's the hammer?
Where's the crowbar?
March ahead with strong steps, O the soldiers,
The front-travelers!

Where are my dear brothers! Get prepar'd!
No more delay, go ahead!
We're the young heroes, fresh with blazing vigor,
We suck the blood and tear
The throat of all obstacles, danger!
The team of youths, we will grow crops and flowers!
March ahead with strong steps, O the Front-travelers!

The vibrant youths of the East,
The heroes and defiant,
O the symbol of humanity, our pride!
I foresee, with proud you march side by side,
Mountains you will cross, deserts and rivers!
On foot march ahead with strong steps the front-travelers!

The tired, decrepit, the ancient nation
Of the East, lost that pride of dedication !
They're immobile, their heads are down,
We will bear that burden, we're the young,

We will take the eternal vow nobly sung,
We will teach them new invocation!
March ahead with strong steps stronger,
O the young travelers!

Leaving behind the rotten past we will move ahead,
Passing the caves and mountain fast,
Sing we will the song in an open valley.
A world we will create with variety, vigor and vitality,
Fresh and vivacious, a great work creat'd newly,
'Tis in motion, voluptuous, lively!
O the team of the creators of the new age,
March ahead with strong steps and rage!

In teams we move in the forests as
Expeditionist, on the river-bank, gorges,
In the water, on the land!
Steadfastly we will cross the steep mountain,
After conquering everything we crush under our feet,
With extreme courage we break obstacle that we meet!
The novice team in an unknown road to tread,
With strong steps march ahead!

A damn we build cutting the dry trees older,
Move forward through the stream of water,
Extreme current difficult to cross over,
At *Rashatal* bottom we dig diamond mine,
In the womb of the virgin earth we create flowers devine,
With foot-steps the earth distance we measure,
March ahead with strong steps, O the restless front-travelers!

Drifting through new stream of the East we've come,

Climb'd down from the peak of the ridg'd mountain owesome,
High plateau we cross'd and channels there,
Tracking the foot-print of a wound'd tiger,
We came out from the bottom of the earth's abode,
The frantic travelers we are on the road!
The travelers- the front-army,
March ahead with steps stormy!

Indebt'd we're to Ireland, Arabs, Korea, China,
Egypt, Norway, Spain and Russia-
Their trace we find in our blood vain!
We all the 'Comrade' of one pain!
To all countries we all belong!
The eternal travelers for the journey long,
March ahead with steps strong!

The reinless, unfetter'd loving youths,
When we behold you our blood seethes!
In pain we cry, but yet your love makes us dance
In ecstasy with a new hope and stance!
The lotus goddess of destiny you're,
O the soldiers! The front-travelers,
March ahead with steps stronger!

O the young ascetic! Be stronger and passionate!
Open up the door of a dreadful, not the door of a compassionate!
The motherland— snake-fang'd, arms-bearing woman,
Hoist her flag that you can!
'Tis your blood-thirsty unwavering cruel penance instead!
O soldiers, with strong steps march ahead!

Listen! The fearless, worry-free young men who venture,
Behind us shout the animals and vultures!
The rotten old melt'd corpses glare,
The aged conservatives eulogize those corpses there,
Let the foxes howl, the Shiva is undaunt'd!
O the fearless heroes, with strong steps march ahead!

In the front where soldiers are in the battle to survive,
Dead is replac'd instantly by soldiers who are alive,
Still hope is there, who stops behind? Move forward courageous!
In the battle, in the defeat, move ahead O the soldiers!
Kindle the lamp there,
Kindle the fire!
The Front-travelers, O the soldiers to tread!
With strong steps march ahead!

In the veins of the timid earth the pulsation arises anew
For our sake with a hope new!
They're ours, with firm stride who move ahead
Alone or in hundreds!
We're strong and firm
With thousand strong arms!
O the sentries of the never-ending night full of dread!
With strong steps march ahead!

In this multifarious procession of the earth 's norms,
There always a dalliance of panorama and forms !
Those coal-smeared *cooli*, the *sharongs* of the ship,
Peasants with plough and oxen stricken with grief,
The grinding-machines — servants, the master,

The stoic front-travelers,
March ahead with steps stronger!

The oppress'd, world's unreveal'd frustrat'd lovers,
The smitten dignity of all the prisons' prisoners,
All the destitutes of the world, happy and honest,
All the dead, alive and dishonest,
Lost they're not,- they're wayfarers,
They're all our companions. O the soldiers, front-travelers,
March ahead with steps stronger!

The revolving wheel of light throws the discus,
Behold! The constellation of planets, the auspicious
Sun and stars glow brightly,
The day is full of light and bright and lively,
The night is dreamy,-
All are looking at us friendly,
Nearer they're but seems to us still afar!
We're all one northern star,
Overwhelm'd! O the team of new travelers,
March ahead with steps stronger!

All with us, they're ours;
They're our friends, our co-travelers,
Day they're, our
Night they're!
The road just built for the future travelers,
In this procession we're the courageous front-travelers!
Making the slippery road walkable, O the soldiers,
Front-travelers,
March ahead with steps stronger!

O the young girls of the East, the belov'd daughters,
Calling you your companions! O the wives, O the sisters!
Since you're not with us, humiliat'd today we're!
Let your gem-ston'd anklets produce sounds there,
Move ahead O the lively wanton front-travelers-
Team of youths! March ahead with steps stronger!

O the future minstrel of desert and grass land!
The arrival songs we hear sung by you from all around!
With a fast pace you come towards us!
O the Poet of a foreign land, capricious!
Stop playing your flute under the shadow
Of the banyan tree in a meadow,
End'd in a success your arduous endeavor,
The team of holy minstrels, the front-travelers,
March ahead with steps stronger!

We want not frail dream and delight,
Comfort-cushion, velvety-sandal, or spit,
The message of peace, books of wisdom in a godown,
Evasive desire like fragile spiderweb, cheap reputation,
Rotten wealth, trample them all by the feet!
With merciless sufferings O the team of ascetic,
March ahead with strong feet!

Those gluttons have become frenzi'd in eating,
Drinking and feasting?
Those pot-belli'd gluttons sleep,
Door and windows they keep
Shut with the blind-screen slipp'd down?
Listen O dear friends, course bread, blankets torn,
Floor-sleeping and lentils—

Are our allowances as support incidentals!
O the worshippers of pain,
No more shedding tears in vain,
March ahead, march ahead without strain!

Is it night? That arduous road is endless?
Who stops on the way, unenthusiastic, hopeless?
Nothing to be afraid of, rest a while in road-side mansion beautiful,
If the short stoppage makes them forgetful
Of their strenuous days~let them forget!
Our goal is undaunt'd yet,
The front-travelers, the team vow'd,
Have a courage, march ahead, march ahead!

Listen to that distant sound of bugle horn,
Announcing the tidings of the new dawn!

O you! Make haste! Go ahead, far ahead!
Sing the songs, the front-force, march ahead,
Move fast farther to the front-line in sights!
Get hold of your rights!
Marching on foot, O the gallants of the front!
With strong steps march ahead to confront![Jinjhir]

A few words:
The poet tried to encourage the subjugated men and women of India under the British rule and addressed them as front travelers in his awakening words to move forward with courage, hope and aspiration.

*The Immortal Zoglul**

In the dark night suddenly I hear
A din of uproar at the door
Of the East. The tiger of Egypt, the head
And sword--
All are gone at a time! There
Flows the desert-angel Blue Nile striking her
Head on the banks,
In the mud the oyster pearls drop down
In her *anchal*! Spreading their dishevel braids
The algae swim on the sandy beach in the streams,
Who is that angel comes here riding the palanquin--
The desert *simum*? A sandy screen
The wind holds from both sides,
Undulates the pine branches!
The whirling-slave girls bring wet-*anchal*
From the Blue Nile and spray cold water of clouds!
Is it the Egyptian queen
Unconscious in the palanquin?
From the broken minarets
Of the *Dewani-Aam* a bewailing emanates
In the darkness,
In the fields the cows graze,
Farmers plough'd not today! Water overflows
From the wheat fields, farmers set up not
Earthen ridges around the crop fields,
The ridge around their mind is broken by tears!
How can he hold that water
When a monsoon engulfs the heart, water pours down
From eyes! On the head thunder falls down
On all a sudden!

The common people are crying prostrating down
On the earth! Saying "O mother, the man
Is made of dust, in your womb again
He turns into dust,
Jewels become not dust, on our head
It remains as *Kohinoor*!
Tell him –what more
We can do now! In the time of distress we opened
The door to look for the jewel, will you steal that?
Shall we get back our treasure that was lost?
Touching iron we take oath ~if we find not our
Jewel back, we will flow a blood of river!"

The village girls milk not the cows –
They cry and idle time they pass!
The baby-sheeps are standing afar- they eat not
The grass or drink no milk! The smiles
Of the Egyptian girls,
Their little teeth like sharp knife are
Not lively enough today! The bundles of vine-creepers,
Bunch of grapes like graceful fingers of young girls,
the bun of angel girls- are falling down like tear drops
The angels are worri'd,
The enemies are all around~
Where's the conqueror of enemies?
The anklets the desert-concubines
Threw away while she
Was crying, may be the anklets dangled on the date-tree!
As if the Egyptian mummy has died one more time, the pyramid
Goes down to the grave again to show him due respect!

When there was no leader in Egypt, its people
Manag'd it, the shock of losing Sudan people
Forgot when they found *Zaglul*!
I know not, when the cataclysm will happen,
The dooms day is not colossal than
What happen'd now in Egypt! The Egypt is there
But its unresistable youth has gone for e'er!
Rustam died— Koshru's throne was getting old!
Which curse that made Egypt decrepit
Untimely! Which son of Egypt can give her
Youth back? In the eyes of Egypt there
Remains the deluge of the Swez canal! Sudan
The great gift of God is gone!
The Moses died before the Pharaoh was drown'd
And dead, the night of the East will not end?
The colorful dawn will not rise again?

I heard, when Pharaoh was in Egypt kill'd new born babies
Snatching them away from the mothers' eyes!
The message he heard ~ walking through his own
Royal corridor a yet- to be-born baby is coming to his kingdom
With the message of his death, the one who decried a life
Of a baby is hiding behind others' death; he thinks, he got life!
Fearing the king, in a river the mother drift'd the baby,
Towards the king's *ghat* the graceful baby
Float'd! He came into the lap of the queen, that
Baby grew up day by day—the Pharaoh recogniz'd not
His own enemy who dances o'er his bosom, the one yet-to-come has enter'd
Into his palace through the front door, till that moment

the guards
Were awake and vigilant all over the places, 'tis the whim of God;
His sympathy to anyone who can neglect!

We saw not Moses but we saw you, the Egyptian saint!
We saw not the Pharaoh but saw Pharaoh-style oppression,
The countless soldiers are running! Fearing whom?
The prisoner's shakles are all over – the hang-man with hanging rope,
Death sentence is written on every pages of the law books,
Only to avoid death he keeps
Himself alone, feeding every new born baby with poison
In the name of education, inspiration and civilization,
They're the new Pharaohs in the last age of creation,
They kill the humanity first before they kill the man!

O the superman when did you come in the festival
Of life with the people who have no humanity at all?
The death punishment is all around, there
You came as a daylight, a fearless wayfarer!
There was a royal wall to hide you, you stood there
And fill'd its gap entire!
A unique arm Prophet Moses had sent by God
himself ! Whene'er he would call, appear'd
The heaven-angels began to him! You were not a prophet
–No revelation you receiv'd,
The angel of heaven was not your friend,
No path was creat'd in the river Nile by your command,No mountain greet'd you with *salam*,
Yet the Asia and Africa sing the psalm
Of your glories! Man has powerful entity,

If he has humanity!

You have shown, if fearless is the subservient nation
Even if they have no weapons,
They still can win the battle!
Not by sword, but with fearless heart they will
Win the battle, one can win the battle
With weapons, but not the country! Sea of fear they cross'd
Without bowing down their heads,
Seeing the beast's teeth and nails they never stepp'd back,
By ignoring the frowning of hypocrites
Rakhi of fearlessness they tied on the wrist of the nation,
That tie has tied them by being a garland
Of flower, though he is not a Prophet, God or incarnation,
All men and women of all countries of all time sing
And ask for his blessing!

At the shore of humanity of this India, O the saint,
Millions of sacrificial goats are grazing day and night!
With internal clash between the clans -every day with their blood
The shore of Indian Ocean is colored!
When the king of beasts breaks their necks,
The other one among them is getting fatty and worthless!
I hear and laugh, they have also religion and caste!
They're Ram goat, Brahma goat and petty goat!
Till they're inflicted by the butchers
Each other they castigate raising their fingers!
If their child is killed by a fox, meeting they hold
With moaning! Shame they feel not while saying good
Words, no humanity with them, I know not
How they demand

Chastity from the women!
Long time ago perhaps someone in our generation,
Tasted little bit butter oil, still now we find
Its smell in our hand and still we lick that hand!

A hope we had to see a supermen like you, and all
Of us forget our distress, all the fakes things will turn into
    real!
So, Egypt not only mourns,
Grief spreads over two continents –
Asia and Africa! Hundred times subjugated
India remembered you, in your hand was the gate
Of entrance for the sea-pirates,
The hero of the frontline ! O the hero of 'the people of
    Israel!'
We give the offerings – the tears of *Bhagiroti* in the water
    of Nile!
No time we have to greet you with *salam* lifting two hands
Straight up, what can your *Fateha* give you to this nation
Other than a couple of known words!
Bless us only, so that a little bit
Of sands can fly from your country deserts
To this country of soothing cold breeze and rivers!

In your farewell I remember those days of the distant past,
When Moses took farewell for-ever from Egypt,
The river Nile made a path for him showed respect,
Behind him cried the Egyptian men and women, the
    Pharaoh's soldiers
Jumped in the waves of the river!
Moses crossed it, but the Pharaoh returned not from the
    River Nile!

I will not mourn at your farewell for a while,
Perhaps I will see you tomorrow!
There behind you drown the *Dajjal* and Pharaoh![Jinjhir]

My words:
When a true leader of a country dies, his loss is immense and cannot be recovered. The mournful people of Egypt bemoaned the sudden death of Zaghloul Pasha, the Prime Minister of Egypt on August 23, 1927. Poet narrated the emotional feeling of the people of the Egypt, their wailing and frustration in a country without a leader.

A Timid Lover

I know, why you cannot look back!
Coming out from a nook
Of a house you're today in the temple
Of god. In playing with dolls
You played with yourself in whims,
In the tearful anxious eyes
You knew not
There was a game of heart,
Loving each other is a huge encumbrance,
That momentary eyes-to-eyes
Glancing is not enough!
I know, why you cannot look back!

I know, why you cannot look back!
You knew not,
Eyes can be lost
In eyes; words can be drowned slowly,
No one else was there but you only,
No exterior existed there but only the interior,
Kohl was there in the eyes, but no tears!
Even though that day the deception sounded not
In the jinglings of the anklet in the foot!
I know, why you cannot look back!

I know why you do not talk! Even though that
Day the creepers intertwined not
With the foot on your way to the woods!
Even though that day in bewilderment you plucked flowers,
Your fingers you hurt not while stringing flowers,
You knew not, along with garland of flowers a heart

Was dried up, you knew not, hiding behind that
Talkative mouth a loneliness cried.
I know why you do not talk!

I know your trickery, your cunningness!
You knew not, that cheek has the redness
Like pomegranate juicy seeds,
You knew not, the mind of a timid
Woman is like a creeper loaded with bees~ she shivers,
Her indistinct voice forbids me to touch her,
The more my eyes meet her eyes,
More shyer she becomes,
In shyness only she rebukes me !
I know your cunningness, your trickery !

I know, O the timid! Why is this astonishment!
You never knew someone becomes fearful when
He looks at himself! Man is harsh, that
You knew! The stone you saw but
Prostrated not on it,
At length you prostrated, your tempted
Hands wanted to touch his feet!
You knew not, the heart-stone could turn
Into a touch-stone by friction!
I know, timid! Why is this astonishment!

That I also know why you're scared.
From both sides of the body whispers the hungry heart!
Fragrance of *bokul*'s blooming flowers that petals
Cannot hold, the more you want to hide yourself
The more you become open,
Crowded in your stolen

Glance are those secret words,
That also I know why you're scared!

I know why you can't speak out openly.
The *bulbuli* informed you about his appeal secretly.
How could he know his words you wanted to hear?
Looking at your eyes he told you those words!
Who knew his strong finger could talk magically!
I know why you can't speak out openly.

I know why you're not ornamented,
Pain made your whole body golden!
The goddess of clay is adorned with gold,
Needs to be decorated again with gold?
The endless purity of mind comes out of the body.
Today the pain adores your beauty.
Ornamented you're not, I know why.

I know, they understand you not.
At the night a virgin girl slept,
In the morning she woke up as a wife! For oysters
They swim in the frothy water,
They know not oysters sink at the bottom!
In the oyster the pearl is formed,
In the tears of eyes the oyster is drowned,
O the unfortunate woman,
How can you make me understand —
How heavier a load is needed for a heart to sink?
[Jinjhir]

My words:
Poet described his shy and timid lover with all her pain she is

laden with.

Her shyness and timidness are adorned with her beauty. The pain she concealed was bloomed like flower petals. That fragrance of pain the petals could not hold. That heart loads so much pain. So heavier is the load of pain... that can sink!

A Row Of Betel-nut Trees By My Window

Good-bye, O my night awakening companions by the window!
O my friends, the parting night is getting pale like a shadow!
As of today at the window moonlight will not shimmer,
No more our silent intimate conversation would be there...

Keeping her chin at the window of the setting
Sky the moon cries,~'O the traveler, there ends
The night, open your eyes !'
Into the shadows of far-off woods the night walks—
Looks behind again and again in drowsiness she stoops,
The tousl'd hair of darkness she entwines with her hands.

I woke up, startl'd, on my forehead someone breathes?
Who fans the wind? Near my head who stays
Awake? The dream walker there I find —
My late night companion!
The row
Of betel-nut trees by the window!

With each other we talk'd through our eyes all night long,
Do you recall that O my companion?
When I was awake and alone, my eyes were irritat'd
And turn'd watery, then like cold
Palms of my belov'd your leaves touch'd
Me! As if the murmuring of your leaves is an aggriev'd
Appeal of her voice! I saw the dark lines
Of her kohl in your leaves,

Her tall body-curves are like yours!
The low murmurings in your leaves are her
Bashful words, 'tis her *sari's anchal* that hangs o'er
From your branch! – You fan the breeze like
The affectionate touch of her finger!

With all these in my mind I fell asleep
And dreamt a dream deep~
Near my bed swings the bluish fringe forthwith,
In the dream again you came and left me with
A kiss on my warm forehead!
My hand in my dream I stretch'd
To you but in embarrassment I pull'd
It back and touch'd the window instead!
My friend, that window now ought to be clos'd!
The travelers are awake, they cry out aloud,~
'For the journey be prepar'd!'

~Today, before our parting from each other
So many wishes in my heart appear—
To know you and to be known!
The words of your heart I condone,
Why this greedy mind wants to know then
Some words of the heart that are only spoken?
I know, through words we will never be known,
In our hearts the *vina* will play only the pain!

I treat'd you the way perhaps I was not
Suppos'd to! O dear, it matters much to you if my heart
Is content'd? If my tears make you elegant?
If love can create the *Tajmahal* charming
With the lost *Mumtaj*, O dear, what's the harm in

It? For you a home I shall not decor at all,
I'll create for you a heaven blissful!...

May be a smaller branch has never met a branch bigger,
From the bushes the cuckoo never coo'd in your
Garden to uphold the appeal of leaves in the voidness!
You kept yourself awake in the night, no one else
Stay'd awake with you keeping the window open!
I was the first to come, with you I stay'd awake all night long;
With you I fell in love fore'er,
On your leaf I wrote my first love-letter!
Whether I see you or not, let it be my consolation! ...
Longing for you my friends,
I won't stay awake anymore, any body's meditation
I'll not break making hue and cry all day long,
Calm and quiet I'll be, within myself I will burn alone
Like a bereft sweet-smell'd incense.

Though I shouldn't, yet I ask before I leave~removing that lattice
Of leaves did you also look at me with the same feelings
I had in my heart as I look'd at you while opening the window?
Was it the breeze or my love made your leaves undulate though?
When in your yellow *anchal* the moon will sleep? Being swoon'd
In deep happiness,~on that occasion of illumination
Will you remember that guest who appear'd in your life for a while?
In this lone room loudly your breath will bewail?

That night O dear, the light of the moon will be annoying
To your eyes? Opening the shutters will you look at the setting
Zone far away? Or in this way will you be standing
In meditation for all day long?

O the helpless tree, tied you're firmly with the land, dust
Beneath your feet, above, the heat of sky-desert!
Burnt you're by the heat of sun, at night you're wet by dew,
Have no strength even to cry, deadly opium made you
Drowsy! If your pain inflict you not, O my friend, no need
Of giving me back my pain from your heart void !
If I come ever by mistake in your remembrance,
Forget me! By mistake if my window is left open,
Close it again!...Whom you find
Not on the land look not
For him in the dark sky
Through the lattice.
(Chakrabak)

A few words:
In this poem the Poet narrated his feeling, passion and emotion in superb poetic skill. He sees a row of betel-nut trees as his night awakening companion, as his lover. He talked to her, expressed his feeling to her and at the end he bid her farewell, saying... the first love letter he wrote on her leaf.

A Wayfarer

I know not my destination, where I'm heading for,
A wayfarer I'm, O brother, a flowing river
In between two banks
Of happiness and sorrows!
On my own way I flow, creat'd
From the peak of a mountain, day and night
Restless,
Changing my course in many places!
My own home has become a home to others, zigzag
Way I took through mountains just after my birth,
I never went back home,
An absconding child I'm,
Born in the womb of a mountain-daughter,
Before she took me into her bosom instantly I left her!

Forgetting its mother the path the fawn takes to run away
While listening to a flute, the path the rabbits take to flee away
While listening to the murmur of the falls, the path the birds
Take to fly towards the endless sky leaving the nests,
The path the newly born clouds take to move towards the sky
From above the sea— I took that path to flee away!
From that day on I run through the mountain, caves,
Fields and paths, hundreds of straight and curv'd alleys
In the villages,—detaching from the planet I move like a meteor,
Climb up the stairs of heaven! I know not where
I'm flowing to, they build their homes on of my banks,
I came to their banks from that hill, they think!

Their wives take pitcher-full-of-water from me,
They say, 'What a relief from the heat!' while bathing in
    me,
They felt only my coolness, they watch'd not the fire
In some places on my banks, it flam'd many funeral pyres!

Ah! So many unfortunate women died,
How many I know not,
While they came within my reach they all drown'd!

The sounds of anklets of the village wives
Tinkle in many *ghats* on my banks,
Their sweet jinglings echo'd in the waves of water.
The flute the shepherd boy play'd sitting under
A tree on my bank, on me reflect'd the far-off moon,
I know, I know, from both my sides with affection
They call me, those lotus-fac'd women there
Call me, 'Stop, let's make a home here!'

But I run and flow with babbling sounds,
Listen not to a house-wife somewhere around
Makes a whistling sound from her mouth on a festive
Occasion, the merchant-daughter in the boat
With full load of gems floats over me, I keep moving away
    from
The boat with the sound of murmuring streams.
The creepers and grasses cover'd my banks in vain,
They watch'd not my turbulence but my inner pain!

Here comes at night secretly the unfortunate girl
To my bank, I tell her through the rippling,
'O the girl, I know you!' go away from the bank, instead

Of dying in the river!' to this day a home-abandon'd
Flute looks for you all-o'er
My banks! she jump'd into the river,
But on my own course I moved on —
At the sand-bottom of my memory
One day lost she will be!

Alas! I know not I move towards an unknown
Attraction, the more I move, the more frequent
Murmurings come out from the deep water, restless
I move forward, no time to pause,
I ruin anything I touch- a thing is here
Now, after a while- 'tis not there,
A home is here,
In the next moment it exists no more !
O you river, move ahead
With your rippling sound,
Do you need to look back ? That female wild duck
From your side calls the male duck!

In the evening on the banks to their nests
They return, they pick up my scatter'd smiles
From the mud in their *anchal*, with the corpse
Burning in the pyre I stay awake on my banks,
But they leave! the whirling pain gets twist'd in my heart
And murmurs! O the rippling flood-water, move fast!
Here the mud-water makes you more
Turbid relentlessly! salty tear-drops you'll not find here,
Move forward, O the wayfarer!
For you the salty seven seas are longing there!
[Chakrabak]

A few words:

A river is restless and moving from one place to another witnessing many things around him without knowing the destination. The poet's life is like a river. He is wanton and wandering around. He is moving and moving to reach a place where an eternal life is longing for him!

Behind The Song

My song I left in thy voice~
Our intimacy will live only in the song? Futile is everything else?
In the deepest bottom of heart the pain that long'd,
Couldst thou discern that pain hidden behind the song?

May be I sang the song only, talked seldom perhaps,
The message of song is luxury only, its ardency is false?
When my heart is full and overflow'd,
In my voice that fullness echo'd,
Tingl'd frequently~the tone of my song thou didst hear
From a far-off shore,
The meaning of song thou couldst not
Grasp at all? That tone shook thy heart
Or
Simply it dangl'd like an ear-ring in thy ear?

Ah! I cannot think—
The moon that creates the tidal wave in the sea
Hearken'd not the sobbing of the sea
Echoing day and night from shore to shore relentlessly?
Behind the song cries that melody,
That *vina* it hearken'd not?
Touch'd not thy heart
The fragrance of the garland
Of my songs? Those words of my heart turn'd

Into a hanging rope in the neck around?

O my belov'd, forget not~ flower that

Dri'd up in the morning put it not
Back into a vase of flower in the evening!
The rose that doth bloom in thy garden in the morning
I know, to it thou dost go nearer
To have its grace and smell sweeter!

The flower that bloom'd in the thorny creepers with bleeding profuse,
All o'er the branches its wailing of the life is induc'd—
Seest thou not that flower? Flowers didst thou want to make a garland
Of union! In the rattle of my pain thou hadst play'd a clattering sound!
Forget my songs, 'tis of no use keeping little bit of acquaintance,
I'm none of thine heart but only a necklace in thy voice!
If I were to ask, thee I only ask—
Did I get nearer to thy heart overtaking thy voice?
[Chakrabak]

A few words:
The deliverance of melodious songs and music of the poet to his lover will be futile if she does not get the pain, passion and desire that is hidden in the heart of poet behind the songs.

'Tis My Pride

Even though I haven't gotten that garland of thy neck
In my neck,
I'll design thee- 'tis my pride!
Sweet heart, with such eyes those who behold
Thee, in their visual perception thou art
What thou art!
In my dream, in the seat of my mind—
With whole splendour thou art my queen!

When everyone around thee will make lot of commotion,
Far away song of praise I'll write for thee in a world of meditation!
My *urbashi* of music I'll compose at the bank of *suradhuni*,
In the voice of many
Thou wilt dangle by being the garland of songs again—
O the tearful Poet's lover with deep pain!

When I will be no more with thee, my songs will be,
Everyone there will ask, 'Who is she?
Did she make Poet's heart to cry?'
Sleepless thousand stars will gaze thee from the sky,
At night thou wilt stay awake with thy friend,
Look at the sky, recall me indistinctly in my song!
Tearfully thou wilt say with pain in thy heart
'O dear ! Who's she? Is she that fanci'd belov'd
In thine song? Around thee they will laugh and sing,
With tearful eyes thou wilt look for thy own-self sitting
In seclusion
With a new outlook- in my poems, in my songs!

When this world will fail to hold thee,
Forgotten thou wilt be shortly,
In the tears of my songs,
In the lotus petals of my words, swing
Thou wilt, the everlasting, the youthful e'er!
No *vina* will be there that day, only my words will resonate there!

Even though I haven't gotten that garland of thy neck
In my neck,
I will design thee – 'tis my pride!
In my tears, in the deceitful melody of my ballad,
In my language, in my pain and torture,
In my poetry, thou callest me in gesture,
O my lover fore'er!

I won't take thee to heaven,
Down to the earth at thy feet the heaven I'll bring
To make thee forgetful of the world!
High above thee— thou art the goddess unfurl'd,
Will it be worthwhile of me to adore that beauty?
From the goddess I want no mercy
But my lover's tears I seek,–
Tears that tumble for little bit of pain, for little bit of pique!

With the dolls the way in childhood thou hadst play'd,
Wedding of a clay-doll cheerfully thou hadst arrang'd!
The house in the sand thou hadst built
With an affection for the dust in thy heart,
Then, there was no heaven, no sun, star and moon,
Likewise thou wilt play again and put me in the trap of illusion!

Inside a clay-made hut a lamp of clay thou wilt kindle,
With color of happiness thou wilt turn a fistful
Of dust into gold !When the half moon in the sky rise proudly,
Thou, the rest half of the moon, wilt appear smilingly,
With thine bun the lightning will entwine happily!

Thou art my *bokul juthi,* a clay star-flower therein,
O the first moon of *Eid* is thine Persian ear ring!
My queen, that flowery color'd *sari*
Thou wilt wear in the darkness of *chaiti,*
In the sky-river there rises the tide of colorations,
At the gate will be play'd pathetic *baruan multan*!

With the same melody of my own compos'd lyric someone
Unknown will knock at thy door and seek for thy love at the day's end!
Sitting in the courtyard in a colorful evening
A good many will desire thee, but my longing
Love will be conceal'd in their desire!—'Tis my pique all along,
Those who ask for thy love—for them I'll write the song!

Even though thou didst not appear in my world's courtyard,
From a musical *shayambar* thee I conquer'd!
Profusely by thine splendor my world was illuminat'd,
'Tis needless to know~ for whom garland thou stringest,
Thy garland I string, 'Tis my pride!
[Chakrabak]

A few words:
The lover of the poet is like a goddess to him. He wants to bring

the heaven down to her feet. Poet's love, his tears, pain, torments, his language, his poetry and melody she perceived in her heart and yet she expressed them silently in gesture.

Even though the poet did not receive the garland of love and melody of his sweet heart on his neck, he expressed his strong desire that he would design her by the melody of his songs the way he wants to. And it will be his pride. He will string for her a garland of love with melody. And it will be his pride again.

The Departure Of Monsoon

O the angel of Clouds! How far will you go?
Made of screwpine tree your boat is tied at the *Ghat* though,
O the momentary, finish'd you your love tryst with the sky
   of east?
Do you recall which land you found least
New and strange more
At the first *Vadar*?

Pollens of screwpine flower are not sleek
For not getting the touch of your cheek,
The bamboo flute bemoans while recalling
You from the bank of the river of *vadar* brimming,
The dew-drench'd *shefali* flowers drop
Like a virgin's tears of love
With her pain of loneliness
In such incomparable dawn's ambience!

O the black girl, the stoical sky looks at your face
With tears in eyes!
In the patches of clouds as white as flowers of catkin
The sail is hoist'd high amidst the stoical wind.
O the girl of the land of water!
The mane like stamens of the *Kadam* flower
Drops on your parting path since the morn!
The buds turn into creepers by your affection,
All day and night long they cry,
Entwine them around the tree!
Flew away somewhere the nightingale bird, but the woman
At home calls the bird in vain through the window again,
The glass full of *chapa* is broken, the thirsty bee came

hurri'dly
But flew away to the land of lotus sadly.
Far away you'll go alone,
The brimming river of *vadar* roars in its tearful tone!
When far away you go at the peak of snowy mountain,
O the angel of clouds, recalling someone will you not feel pain?
Snow's heard, water nowhere,
Only cruel whiteness exists there -
Who knows which one is more soothing -
Pain of estrangement or a holiness pleasing!

Smile not the creepers and trees at the highest peak of glory,
There, the night's *Rajanighanda* remains fresh in the morn early.
Taking off the monsoon-*nupur* from clamorous feet you go there,
Startle not while you walk, dangles not your chignon of hair!
There, an ascetic you will be in meditation deeper,
In cherishing the hope of your coming o'er
Cries the pied-crest'd cuckoo down here!
[Chakrabak]

A few words:
Poet compared the pain of departure of monsoon with the pain of loneliness of a virgin girl, her tears drop like dropping of jasmine in the ambience of dawn. She is the angel of clouds to poet who reaches the highest peak of mountain. Taking off the nupur from her clamorous feet she walks, she walks when her chignon does not dangle. Poet wants to know- does she feel pain when she is alone at the mountain-peak? Where she is in meditation like an ascetic!

I Sing The Song Of Praise

I sing the song of praise for the youth who march'd
Out in all directions for a hard
Expedition holding a sharp sword
In hand with brag and pride!
Their history of destruction
Those who wrote down
On the wall of the thousand years old
Mommy's pyramid,
By their breath those who blew out the dri'd up pages
Of the dilapidat'd scriptures,
Those who broke down the temples,
Abodes of the evil gods
And a wine shop ancient
Of a decrepit hypocrite,
Those who took away the old trashes, huge stones of purification
And the stacks of scriptures by their life-stream down!
Fearlessly in the worshiping places those who appear'd
With the terrible illusory-mallet,
Those who hammer'd the wall of China of restriction and prohibition
By both hands with extreme bravery and ambition!
All the dead bodies and skeletons those who threw away
From the cemetery and made it a fair of flowers' array,
Those who made today the beach of the life vibrant with their crowds!
I sing the song of praise for them who mov'd forward
In this life of the world!..

That night I see~

The traveler who sail'd the boat alone in the turbulent sea
And return'd not to the shore in the morn!
In tearful eyes I stay awake and still write the song
For that brave one all night long!
I still remain awake for him and sing the song .
The one who return'd not
In the morning flew in the sky at night—
The arrow shooter of a new world, the eternal traveler!
Being fearful of him remains vigilant the door keeper.

Those who chase the death every time amidst the agonies of life!
At the bottom of sea, all o'er the horizon, in the endless sky,
From the bottom of *jaskapuri* those who procure jewels,
From cobra's hood withstanding venom jewels they steal!
Those who took the thunder of *bajrapani* on their heads and
Made the flippant cloud-daughter a slave obedient-
Those who made the wind obeisant to flap the fan on them,-
Here I'm to salute them, I sing the song of praise for them.
In their worlds my wailing roars ~
The hanging rope is tir'd enough to choke their throats!
In their prison last night arriv'd a female prisoner,
Shattering the sleep of the dawn she burst into laughter!
[Sandya]

A few words:
Poet sings the song of praise for all invigorated youth of the world. He salutes them. He feels pain for those young men and women who died while doing all heroic deeds to accomplish their goals.

I Sing The Hymn For Those

I sing the hymn for those
Who brought the summon of crops
To the earth, who had scars in their palms for their laborious
Work, receiv'd a dish-full of fruits
And floral tribute from the earth timorous;
Those who made this terrible earth of wild beasts
And dying decrepits a place of charm and grace!
Those who made fearlessly their homes
With wild tigers, pea cocks, lions and snakes in caves!
Those who came with invincible speed and spirit
Like Bedouins, sang the song of love— like Jesus Christ,
Son of Mary—their spiritual touch made
The earth rotate like meteors with speed!
Those who reviv'd the forest from callously destruction
To create paradise there and brought them back into briskness again,
Those insolents who climb'd up the Himalaya out of their
Emotion of life, went to the ocean to suck up its water!
Those who make expedition to the desert in search of a new world,
Tying wings with their body those who soar upward,
Still unstoppable is their invigorat'd speed,
In exultation they fly towards moon, towards planet
Mars, into the endless sky and more!
Those who sell the commodities of life from the door to door
Of death, and lose their stake on life in the battle field
Terrible— I, the desert-poet
Sing the hymn for those *Beday* and Bedouin!

Those who make the revolutionary expedition
In every epoch blatantly,
Those who drink the poison willingly
In the abundance of life, in extreme happiness spear they put
Into their chest!
Those who ignor'd all obstacles
Like the impetuous speedy mountainous falls
Of monsoon, those who are rebuk'd
By the mean-mind'd
As barbarians, took the blame
To be intemperate, I write the song for them,
O I sing the hymn for them!
[Sandya]

A few words:
The poet sang the hymn for the working indigent people, courageous and great men of the world. The hymn is for those who were unjustifiably castigated and condemned in the society.

March Ahead

Chorus:
March, March, March!
High above in the sky the drum-beat resonates,
Restless is the earth down
Here, O the youths of the morning sun,
March ahead, March,
March, March, March!

Hurling a blow on the door of dawn
A dazzling morn we will bring,
The dark night and obstacles all
To the height of *Bindhyachal* dispel
We will! Singing the song
Of the new and young
The crematorium we will rejuvenate,
Induce a new life, new strength in arm!
March ahead, O the young men!
Attentively listen
To the the call of life from every
Death-archway, from every
Door! Crush the bolt of the door such,
March ahead, March,
March, March, March!

Chorus:
From above the thunder commands —
Dress up, O the soldiers
Of the day of Eid, the parade goes on everywhere—
The *Nid-mohal* you open up there!

Reign'd long time ago those capricious Emperors!
Looking back in the past O the travelers,
When you sing a song drop some tears!

Let the thrones and kingdom be abolish'd,
O you wake up, your sense is vanish'd!
Look there! Like Rome, Greek, Russia
And Persia—
So many lands have fallen!
But they all have risen again,
Wake up O the strengthless people!
In the dust we will build up anew the *Tajmohal*!
March, March, March all!
[Shandya]

A few words:
Poet wrote this patriotic chorus song for the subjugated youths of the nation to march forward to achieve victory from the subjugation, to liberate the country from the hand of the tyrant ruler.

The Wave Of The Youth

A sand barrier can hold the wave of youth?
The moon has risen in its zenith,
Who will now stop the tide?
In the sea a deluge emerg'd –
Because the moon was flar'd,
The moon rises not for the canals,
Ponds and jheel,
They remain stand still!
The deluge is all over in the sea of life,
In the fields, in the ghats, in the roads alike,
While sitting on the old branch of a tree let
The vulture curse the flood as much she wants!
O the *Sharosh, Moral*, come, fly over here!
In the waves of flood your nest was drift'd afar,
With those destructive waves you swing and jump up there.

From the banks the vultures
Turn the neck as they watch the fast moving muddy water,
In the dump of melt'd corpses, they eulogize those death!
They're the carrier of senile death,
Seeing their fierce eyes –
O the morning birds!
Songs of virtue will you sing?
They guard all restriction,
They belong not to God, but to destiny!
They're the unbelievers; suck the life-blood of many!

Say, you're the flash-flood of new life!
Let it be muddy in strifes!
From this water e'er-youthfulness the earth has gotten!

It has turn'd the earth to blue from brown!
Those who nurture the killer-germs making barrier around,
Do they know water moves towards sea?
Blind-fold'd they're, immobile like a stump of tree;
They're frenzi'd, animals, inside the caves they live,
No light of dawn of northern sky
They need, living in the dark cave the owls cry
When they see light, let them cry!
The song we will sing, still out there many crows
To kill them! At the end of their life while
Listening to the call
Of morning prayer if they revile,
Pay not heed to them for a while!
Their graves are being dug in the time's graveyard,
In our colorful musical party of the invigorat'd
Life invitees are not those decrepits and dilapidat'd!

With a chain in the leg well wrought
A parrot sings whate'er words he was taught,
O the bird of sky, fly high up and create a new tone of song
In your voice! To the higher sphere you belong,
Let them throw mud from the bottom,
Smearing black shoots from kerosene pots no one
Can fade the brightness of the moon!
Let the wild boar throw mud,
You're the lotus far away from that mud!
Give them the fragrance,
They're the flock of beasts, you're the flowers!

On your clean body filthy mud they throw,
'Tis their habit throwing mud at you!
O the children of heaven, endure that with forbearance!

Branches bring fruits and flowers, birds sing the songs,
Nests they build o'er there,
The people of the bottom are stone-thrower,
'Tis not a humiliation to the trees!
Some monkeys break down branches of flowers,
Ah! In amusement they jump!
We, the human being, are asham'd of it! Crazy they become
For the wounds and sores they have in the heads,
O the youths, blame not them for their deeds!
Not worthy 'tis for being grumpy on an old man though,
Whose funeral prayer will take place tomorrow!

By virtue of the sword you'll bring back a throne of truth!
By killing a mice insult not that sword,
Their time is over! Deforesting a forest a city
They build, if any branch of trees gives scratches on your body,
Just tolerate my brother,
In your hand an axe is there!

Through ages the world is rul'd o'er by the proud
Youths- that rule they never accept'd,
The rule of moribund old men!
A new world we shall create, sing the new song,
The bow'd-down world will accept
Our palm-full of offerings with respect!
Through ages - we, the young, have buri'd those moribunds,
Let them scold us, we will smile on them and say in turn—
'To God we belong, and to Him is our return!'
[Sandhya]

A few words:

Poet was delighted to see the young generation who woke up against all evil and malignant people of the society. No one can hold the wave of the youth that swelled up already. He urged them to shoulder the responsibility of the society from the decrepit elderly people. To him the youths are like birds to fly up, a blooming lotus in the mud and the deluge in sea.

The Blind God Of The Nativeland

Holding the hanging rope in his hand
The blind god comes out slowly from his nativeland,
The foot-print of the travelers and the stain'd
Blue mark on the forehead of the vanquish'd of the past
He followed!

With dense clouds the sky is cover'd all
Around, dark night impenetrable!
In the hand of the foggy horizon
The light is blown out,—the stray'd blind
God walks slowly when
Darkness spreads out! He walks on that road where
Skeletons are scatter'd all over!

The enemy strikes him with the stick of infliction,
With that stick he walks, he made it his companion,
Step by step, slowly the blind god walks~
On his way he fac'd more troubles,
On the road he fell down,
In his chest hold him strongly a young man!

Inside the dark prison all prisoners are awoken,
Wherein everyday the killing-stage is drench'd with blood
    crimson!
Wherein crush'd are the souls with cruel fists,
On the head of snake in the dark cave the jewel dazzles,
In the cave the hungry young men stay awake with
The wild beasts with nails and teeth,
Wherein women for sacrificial offerings offer their lives,
The blind god walks by that path, he walks and cries~

'O you wake up, wake up quickly, the colorful dawn being
Stain'd with your blood has appear'd, —the night is ending!'

The traveler walks in the darkness
Of night towards the destination aimless,
Knowing not which way to go, where to go,
From how far above the god calls though!
Knows he only that a call he heard!
The idle foot gets energiz'd—
The road is open ahead!
That much he has seen!
If there is any quicksand, mountain,
Or vast open desert he cares not much!

In the dark night of the new moon the traveler walks ahead,
With him too the road moves ahead,
He fell down on the road, gripp'd the hand of god.
There —the death, the young man, the blind god
And the smile of the dawn stride
Side by side!
[Sandya]

A few words:
The poet depicted the blind god as a leader of the nation who was not so strong but came forward to help the nation, the young man represented the young generation and the aimless traveler appeared as a bewildered nation who did not know what to do, but they all saw the smile in the dawn of nation. They could walk hand in hand in the road to reach the destination in the darkness of night that shrouded the nation.

Luffa flower

Luffa flower! Luffa flower!
In the land of green bower
You're drongo with turquoise color ~
Luffa flower!

In the shrubs, in the foliage,
In the ear of the creeper-leafage,
Dangles your loveliness with golden shower~
Luffa flower!

In the land of leaves you're the bird around,
With the peduncle your heart is bound,
In the eve your song I listen when you bloom profound!

At the end of the winter-day wearing saffron-yellow attire,
On the land of dried up scaffolds you're the occupier~
Luffa flower!

O the gold- faced little girl in green-mother's lap,
In the sun-drenched noon you fall in a nap.

The butterfly keeps calling you to talk—
'Come here, get detached from the stalk.'
The stars in the sky say~'Come here,
In our boundless sphere!'
Luffa flower!

You say, 'The earth I love,
I want not the kingdom of riches above,
Contented I'm here, though I lost my trail for ever',

Luffa flower!
[Jinghe fool]

A few words:
Like this colorful luffa flower one might love this world of his own and wants to live there. He has no desire for a land of wealth where he does not belong to.. he is contented here in this world.

In Bangladesh the local name of Luffa is Jhinga. It is a vegetative plant under the Family Cucurbitaceae. Luffa grows abundantly in Bangladesh. Its scientific (botanical) name is Luffa acutangula. The genus Luffa has five accepted species, widely cultivated as vegetative plant. It is commonly known as ridged gourd. It has brilliant yellow colored flowers that attracted Poet to write this poem.

In dictionary the jhinga is described as cucurbitaceous plant. All cucurbitaceous plants belong to the family Cucurbitaceae. The family Cucurbitaceae consists of approximately 125 genera and 960 species.

A Little Girl And A Squirrel

Squirrel! O Squirrel! Guava you eat?
Eat molasses, parched-rice, milk, Gourd?
Pomelo?
A kitten? Puppy too?

A glutton, a witch you are, whatever
You find eat alone, all the delicious pomelos down there!
Tail keeping upward still you look around, what for?
A food-greedy! Go away, my friend you aren't anymore!

Squirrel! Monkey-faced!
Shall I strike you with my fist—
Call my older brother? With stones he will pelt you,
Give me a guava, will you?
Go away you worthless!
That's why a flat nose you possess!
Owl-eyed! Fatty definitely!
Eat alone everything hurriedly!
Suffer you'll from stomach disorder!
In your face leper-buds will be all o'er!
O God! Into its belly let one insect enter!

Shsh... eat not that big one, the one ripen!
A lot of guava I love to eat, give me one!
O squirrel ! Want to be my younger sister?
My sister-in-law? My older sister?
Then, give me a guava please! O god,
You're stark naked?
Will you take my frock? Two if you want?
Eat no more guava then,

Stop eating pomelo too, showing your
Teeth you want to run away? O mother,
Come here! ~
Go away! You Squirrel!
Nothing you get at all!
[Jinghe fool]

A few words:
The Poet has shown his extreme poetic skill to put a touch of life in the poem where we see a little girl talks with the squirrel who is eating the fruits that she loves most from her garden with deep dejection and dissension.

The Snub-Nosed Grandpa

O mother! Who kick'd on your father's nose?
There the blunt-nos'd dances with his snubb'd nose,
~ *Deng- deng!* The dent'd-nose!

Who fil'd his nose to make it snubb'd?
As if he is a baby titmouse with its tail downward!
Like a bull-frog he is on the back of an old cow!
O mother! Laughter I can't check now!
Deng- deng! The dente'd-nose!

A swab who pricks into his snubb'd-nose!
Chordi says,~awful! 'Tis mucus of his nose!
Like a turtle he lies with his belly upward
And legs sideward!
O mother!
I convulse with laughter!
Deng- deng! The dent'd-nose!

Mother! Grandpa is Chinese,
Chang-chu his name? That's why his nose
Is flatten'd like a moon! A Japanese
Notice on his nose he post'd, O mother!
I convulse with laughter,
Deng- deng! The dent'd-nose!

O mother, grandpa was not a bet-nos'd before!
In his sleep loud sound he makes more
With that flatten'd nose like seven conchs!
So with a big slap grandma dent'd his nose!
O mother!

I convulse with laughter,
Deng- deng! The dent'd-nose!
The little joyous baby-mongoose jumped
And stuck in the mesh of beard!
The nasal-ton'd kitten wants to go Delhi! O mother!
I convulse with laughter,
Deng- deng! The dent'd-nose!

Grandma broke grandpa's nasal bone
While nailing an almanac on his nose?
The cobbler tann'd my grandpa's nose!
O mother!
I convulse with laughter,
Deng- deng! The dent'd-nose!

Mother, sometime nasal-ton'd has a nose upright,
Take grandpa there for his smiles at the first sight.
For the god *gorur* meditation grandpa start'd,
Flat-nos'd grandpa wants to be a long-nos'd,
Deng- deng! The dent'd-nose!
[Jinghe fool]

A few words:

This amusing doggerel verse the poet wrote where we find a young boy wants to know from his mother why his grandfather is snub-nosed and thus he makes fun out of it constantly.

The young grandson brought some examples that he perceived to be most accurate in describing his grandpa's nose in an amusing manner. Here the poet with his immense skill described the mind of the child who loves to make fun.

The Song of Dawn

'Tis now dawn, open up the door,
Wake up O dear
Little girl! The birds are chirping over
From the *Jui*-branch there,
Run O flowery little girl!
Wake up O dear little girl!
The sun there
Crawls up in the sphere
Wearing colorful garb, listen there,
The gate keeper
Sings the songs,~ rama ho! Leaving their
Nests birds fly high,
Together they come nigh,
In the sky they fly...
Endless are their songs,
With the dawn-breeze the songs drift along!
The unrestful
Nightingale
Whistles to flowers, this time,
This time,
The little girl will wake up!
The helm is set up,
Ready to sail up,
There floats
The boat,
This time, this time,
The little girl open'd her eyes!
Not a lazy she is,
In the morning she wakes up,
In every night

On her forehead
The moon puts a *tip*,
They woke up,
They ran out,
All the children around,
'Who woke up first'
Listen to their lively tumults!
The night ends,
Wash your face and hands,
Wake up O little girl! While singing
The song of praise of God, ask for His blessing
With gratification!
[Jinghe fool]

A few words:
The theme of this poem 'The song of dawn' written for the children is centered around the wisdom of remembering God first in the morning. This little girl like many other kids amid delightfulness of a charming morning wakes up with pure soul to follow the day with the praise God.

The Litchi Thief

Near the palm pond of the *Babus*
The greyhound of the *Habus*
Chased me terribly,
'Stop! Stop for a while!' Said I hurriedly,
There is a litchi tree near that pond, you know!
Slowly there I go,
The moment I climbed up the tree
With a big sickle in my hand free,
Its small branch that I gripped around
Broke down with a cracking sound!
I fell down violently
On the neck of the gardener only,
He was hiding behind the tree,
Despicable indeed was he,
With his fist he hit me wantonly, fiercely!
Strongly I slapped him too,
And with speed I managed to run through!
I jumped over a wall,
There I found a jackal!
What! You jackal, get lost from here!
'Twas standing there!
Startled I was at the sight of it,
The dog too started running after me!
To myself I said, 'Now I'm finished',
The dog will bite me before I'm vanished!
In panic loudly I cried out,
Through a hole I escaped!
I entered into the house of *Bose*.
What a relief it was that I can't lose!
Should I go again to steal?

Not at all, I swear, to steal I've no zeal,
How can I forget that dog's scolding!
And beating of the gardener that I'm holding!
What d' you say? Next week again?
No ! I'm regretful with much repentance![Jinghe fool]

A few words:

Poet described a frightful experience of a boy while he was stealing litchi from the tree in a garden owned by someone else. The bitter experience he earned from a chasing dog and ruffian gardener that he could not forget and that made him regretful very much. Usually this childhood adventure happens in suburban or village environment that poet described in a vivid poetic skill.

LYRICS

[1] O Parul, Art Thou Awake?
[Bheempolosri- Dadra]

O '*Parul*', art thou awake? '*Sat Bhai Champa*' calleth thee!
In the gaps of moon-lit clouds thou hast appear'd!
Thou art in a sea voyage for a land
Of illusion of riches,
Where flowers bloom always
In the flowery branch of life! Millions of stars
Look into the window of darkness,
Shattering that prison woke up all female prisoners!
Amidst forgetfulness stay not in the heaven,
Moor thy golden boat at the shore
Of this world,..again at the curve of this river!
[Bulbul]

A few words:
Poet wrote this poem when a lady whom he loved was about to leave Dhaka for England. He fell in love with Miss Fajilutunnessa, a brilliant student who had her Master degree in Mathematics from the University of Dhaka in 1928. The ardent lover-Poet wrote a letter to his friend Dr. M. Hussein," I leave with you the most secret and the tragic leaf of my life. I consider her [Fazilta] the most beautiful woman. My feeling tells me that the one who had declined me in life will accept me in death."

[2] O Nightingale, Swing Not The Flower-Branch

[Bhairabi-kaharba]

O Nightingale, swing not the flower-branch
Today in the garden,
Still in their sleepiness the buds
Teeter in drowsiness!
Oh! To this day blows the northern wind
O'er the empty branches day and night,
The gazal-singing southern breeze is
Yet to come, perplex'd are the honeybees!
When will the flower-princess drop her veil off?
With soothing touch of dew drop
Wake she will up
With blushing cheek!
From the spring's sprouting buds a deluge of flowers will
    bloom,
With dimple in cheeks in buds' lip smile will loom!
O Poet, with sweet smell thou art charm'd,
Finding no shore in water thou art drown'd!
Thy bosom thou hadst fill'd up with flowers,
Today with tears thou wilt fill up thy eyes![Bulbul]

A few words:

For a while Poet forgets the bitterness of life when he finds a joyous life around him like flowers bloomed around, but he reminds him that momentary charm will not last long, tears will fill his eyes soon. He wants to cherish the liveliness of flowers with him for a longer time, so he urged the nightingale not to swing the branch.

[3]. You Call'd Me With An Eye-Beckon

[Jonepuri-Ashabori-Kaharba]

O who are you so compassionate call'd me with an eye-beckon!
The dark-door of the *rangmohal* you ought to open
Since you call'd me then,

Secretly the letter you sent
To the flower garden
In the spring breeze,
Watching that the quail coos from the branch of trees!

Confidante, as harbinger you sent the cyclone
In the *bhaishak* --the storm-pigeon,
In the monsoon the river full of water
Looks at me with hope more!

In the autumn the *sheuli*-bed is wet
With your tears, with your snow-cold
Breeze you touch me, my sleep
You break if I keep the door close,

In an empty *poush* field,
In a lonely path, O the estranged,
You look for me, Oh! In desolation I look for you,
In the middle cries the thirsty sea!

O the bumble bee-poet! Blend with the morning breeze
With the sweet smell of flowers in the trees,

If you want to be there always
At *sishmohal* in dawn's ambience!
[Bulbul]

A few words:
Both the poet and her lover are estranged. He sees her in the spring breeze, in the sheuli flowers that drop and spread in the misty autumn morning, in an empty winter paddy field; he looks for her in his loneliness.

[4] *Sitting In Seclusion*
[Imon-mixed gazal-kaharba]

Sitting in seclusion
Why are you in a lonely mind?
O *gori*, let's go unto the river
To fetch water,
The forest cries there,
There comes the call of rumblings in the waves of water!

The day ends in the wings
Of the geese,
The she-bird hides
In the bosom of her belov'd!
In tearful eyes *Choka-choki* again
Part from each other, from the flute emanates *raga baroan*!

Making a milkyway-parting in the hair
The night sees her face in the moon's mirror,
In the garden-city dances the shadowy dancing girl,
Her creeper like chignon amorously dangles!

'O bride, the sun is setting'~ calls the sister-in-law,
'Let's go to fetch water, if you want to',
It'll be dark, far away the river stands,
In a civic decoration the city decorates!

In the bathing-*ghat* the boatman ties the boat,
Returns the wayfarer to a seclud'd field,
Thinking of someone your day is over,
With tearfull eyes you fill up the pitcher,

O the heartless, someone is entwin'd
With your colorful feet like a garland,
The Poet is in a dilemma as you're,
Whether to keep him on the feet
Or to put around the neck!
[Bulbul]

A few words:
Poet describes the feelings of a lonely girl.

In the evening, in the setting hour of a day when geese are flying, flute emanates a classic raga, boatman ties his boat to go home then a secluded girl sits in a lonely mind with deep pain of estrangement.

[5] How Can I Forget
[Pilu-kaharba-dadra]

How can I forget!
To this day with pain 'tis delineat'd
In my mind!
O my confidante, without
Him in voidness I count
My days and nights! First you stole my mind,
My heart with a knife you stabb'd then!
So much pain, so much deceitfulness!
Yet coat'd 'tis with honey's sweetness!

Confidante, to this day the *chokori* cries
From afar the moon when it sees,
In the clouds the cradle swings,
In the water the goose swims!

There the dangling *kajla* girl under the *bokul* shrub
Flowers she picks up,
With a pitcher on her bent waist
There goes a concubine with heavy steps!

The trees are without leaves,
Hence comes there the tidings
Of flowers, since flowers are dropp'd
Off, the branches are full of fruits!

O Poet, your branch if someone inflicts
With pain, give her flowers as gifts,
If the bees touch not the buds of pain,

The flower-flags would not flutter again!
[Bulbul]

My words:

The estranged poet is longing for his sweet heart eagerly. He hopes that one day she will come back to him like a spring after the leafless, flowerless harsh winter. The poet will offer flowers to his beloved as gift even though she inflicts pain in the flower-branch of his heart. He will withstand the pain of separation like the sting of bee to get the love of his sweet heart.

[6] My Heart Cries
[Mixed Behag-Khambaz-Dadra]

Whom should I tell in pain my heart cries!
With frequent pause the timid heart throbs!

In the blue sky he lives, in the sea of tears
I live, with twenty seven stars' co-wives he roams,
That moon how can I catch
As I'm not an eclipse!

The one whom I consider as the collyrium of my eyes
Washes away in the dream with hidden tears!
That garland someone steals when I keep
Him in my bosom deep,
If I tie him with my bangle in hand,
With the wind he flies away then,
How can I enchant that stoical mind!
[Bulbul]

A few words:
Poet's lover finds no one whom she would tell her pain of love! Poet is stoical and restless. She cannot tie him in her heart with the string of love.

[7] In Tender Breeze, In Shadow Of A Bokul Tree

[Shindhu-Bhairabi-Kaharba]

In tender breeze, in shadow of a *bokul* tree,
Who comes there secretly!
Gazing at the sky all over,
The wind is swirling in the smell of hair!

In the glow of dawn, in the crimson-red evening
Her both cheeks are shining,
The sun and moon dangle like lotus
In the hair of the night, in the mass of darkness,

When foot touches the lip of leaves
The bud shivers, the flower blooms,
In each blinking of eyes,
The day laughs, the night cries!

The garland of planets is in the bun,
With globate stars cheeks are adorn'd,
With flower's thorn she ties
Her *anchal*, on the green grass her handkerchief lies.

In the evening the girl's bangle-bird
Jingles in the forest,
Her life like a golden dream;
With a baby in the cradle she sleeps!

Dangle me with your playful lotus-hand,
O my queen!

Rock my sweet fragrance
With your intoxicating breaths!
[Bulbul]

A few words:
Poet can see his lover who comes secretly in the shadow of bokul tree when vernal breeze blows the smell of her hair, he feels her presence every where- in the glow of dawn, in the crimson red evening. He urged her to rock his fragrance with her **inebriated breaths.**

[8] O The Stranger, Forest-Stoic
[Bhairabi-Ashabari-Kaharba]

O the stranger, the forest-stoic who
Are you playing bamboo
Flute in the forest?
The caressing melody brings drowsiness
In the garden of flowers, in the flowers' face!

The wings of the bumble-bee get doz'd,
The eyes of jasmine are enamour'd
With passion, in deep sleep the full moon
Is in the corridor of the dawn's horrizon!

With a pain of thrill the bashful charming creeper
Shivers, like a garland in a happy dream there
The young bride is entwin'd with her lover!

Waking up all on a sudden in the middle of night,
I listen to the melody of flute playing in my heart,
In the night in bed who knows why she weeps, for that
Melody of the flute!

I string the garland of words in vain,
O Poet! You hide your heart's pain,
The flutist cries in seclusion,
Raga *tori* is restless in his estranged mind!
[bulbul]

A few words:
Poet himself is a stoical, estranged flutist who plays the melody in

the bamboo flute that makes his lover cry in the deep night; the pain of melody thrills the bashful charming creeper, brings drowsiness in the flowers. The poet listens to the melody of flute as if it cries in his heart. His concealed pain cries in seclusion like an agitated raga of tori(a musical mode).

[9] On Which Bank Of My Life The Boat is Moor'd Today

[Khambaj-Pilu-Dadra]

On which bank of my life the boat is moor'd today,
In which golden village!
Why my boat on the lower stream
Wants to go again toward upstream!

Making my sorrows a helmsman
My broken boat I drift'd along
The stream, with eye-beckoning you call
Me, who are you O the dream-angel!

Called me the stormy night
To blow out my light
Of home, who are you O my companion
Of melody, appeared at the edge of my song!

O the golden girl of the golden land,
Will you be the sailor of my boat?
This time drifts away my broken boat towards
The shining kingdom of riches. [Choker Chatok]

<u>A few words:</u>
Poet's wants to anchor his mind-boat on the bank of his life-a life that shimmers with happiness like a golden village. But he cannot drift his mind-boat towards the upstream. He urges his golden girl- his beloved to be the sailor of his broken boat to drift along towards a life full of happiness like the land of oloka.

10] Who Are You O The Charming
[Bhairavi Gazal- dadra]

Who are you O the charming,
In my drowsiness you appear'd! I adore you,
I adore you,
I adore you,
In the rain
Of the monsoon
The chief dancer dances,
Jhamjham jhamjham jhamjham.

Silently you kiss'd my eyes sitting behind my head,
Besotted with passion my body is bloom'd
Like a kadamba flower, pleasing, incomparable!
O my Master, my basket I fill'd with flowers
That I had in my garden and offer'd them all,
Oh! My flowers you pick'd not up, O forgetful!
Unloosing my bun you took away my flower-garland,
I know not in my dream what I told you then,
So you left me. Waking up I cri'd and call'd—
O my belov'd, my belov'd, my belov'd!
[Choker Chatok]

A few words:

It's an overture of deep adoration that comes from the heart of poet's lover. She addressed the poet as Master whom she offered her all love like flowers all she had in the garden, when she woke up she found her beloved master left her alone- may be he was aggrieved for some reason!

[11] Someone Forgets Not
[Mand-Kaharba]

Someone forgets not, someone forgets
The memory of the past,
Someone cries in desolation,
To forget that pain someone sings a song!
In the cold clouds the blaze
Of lightning someone sees,
Someone brings the blossom of flowers
In his dried up vista of bower.
Someone sees thorns in the stalk of lotus,
Someone sees only the lotus!
Someone tramples over the flowers,
Someone strings the garland of flowers.
No more the light one kindles
In his eternal night of despondence,
Keeping the door open someone
Stays awake to watch the new-born moon!
[Choker Chatok]

A few words:
Poet narrated here two contrasting approaches of perception and reaction to the feelings and emotions that emanate in many events of our life.

[12] O My Deep River
Bhatiali- Kaharba]

O my deep river!
Throughout the life I kept myself afloat on your water!

The home I built, deluge took that away,
On the little island I took shelter to stay,
That island you engulf'd any way!
Everything I've lost, floating now I'm through
An endless time on you!

O dear, my home I get back if 'tis shatter'd,
But you shatter'd my heart!
The mind-jewel is hard to get back once 'tis lost,
O that mind when get lost in the ebb-tide,
Never comes back in the high tide!
O the river, your bank when you break,
Its one side you break!
When mind breaks,
Broken are its both sides!
A little island one can never rebuild
On the bank of mind
If it breaks once!
[Chokher Chatok]

A few words:
The deep river was like the pain of indigence the poet had suffered throughout his life. It fragmented his peace and happiness of home and life, it broke his heart. If the bank of mind breaks no one can rebuild an island on the bank of life.

[13] On My Broken Boat
[Bhatiali- Karfa]

On my broken boat embark not my *Shampan*-passengers,
O dear, I ferry myself from one bank to another!
Everything that river water took away from me,
O dear, at the bottom of that river I want to dive!
Here I come to float,
Money I earn not!
In this mirror of water I saw her,
She is no more in the mirror, but the mirror is there!
Desperately in my tears I look for her,
In the water of the river!

With the hope of meeting her again
I wait in the *ghat* with my *Shampan*,
My belov'd is my rosary, I cry for her!
My pupil you took away O the water of eye-river!

O dear, dries up the river-water but revives again,
A man comes back I heard, if he is bound
To an oath! O someone I lov'd, I was driven
Out from my country while drifting along![Chokher Chatok]

A few words:
Poet's broken boat is the poet himself who is utterly dismayed, no one shares his agonies and pain. The river is like his shattered life, that life took away his happiness and peace. The estranged poet is longing for his lover to meet her again at the wharf of his life.

[14] *In Our Next Life*
[Poroj-ektala]

O dear, in our next life each other we will see!
Forget me here, forget me.

In this life what I could not
Tell you, I shall not
Tell you, you too tell me not!

If I love you, beguile me, once again
If I come back inflict me with pain!

Here in the twinkling of an eye dreams come to an end,
In the morning the flowers of the night drop down,
Here dries up the heart for the lack of affection,
Here the ambrosia is full of pain and poison!

Heart becomes worri'd in separation,
Lost we're from each other after the union,
Within a short time we forget each other,
Remember me in the heaven there,
Where love dries not up in the heart ever!
[Chokher Chatok]

A few words:
Thronged with deep feeling of estrangement Poet urged his lover not to tell him the words she saved in her hearts in this world. And he wil not tell her too what he could not tell here. He hopes to meet her in the hereafter. In this short life the happiness of union and pain of separation also last for a while. Poet wants to be remembered by his lover in the heaven where love is eternal.

[15] The Pact

Chorus—
The *badna* and *garu* are in deep intimacy, a secret
Amour of the new pact!
In the hands of Muslim click no knives,
No bamboo stick in Hindu's hands!

Tiki and beard are tied together like a knot of the sari
And scarf of the bride and bridegroom in the wedding cheery,
A tight fastening with a loose knot? It happens in a hurry!
Forward someone wants to move, the other pulls him backward,
Tighten'd will be the knot by pulling each other awkward!
Unit'd together they're not by heart, but by the back,
That's alright until they crack!
"Where is my *dada*?" Asks *Miah*,
The *Babu* asks, "Where is my brother *Miah*?"
Babu smears dye on *miah*'s beard,
Miah anoints oil on *Babu*'s head,
They look each other obliquely, what a sweet union!
Babu says, "To appease you I eat meat that is on prohibition!"
Miah says, " Each other friendly we will treat,
If you give me two more pieces of that meat!
O *Dada*! Our chicken is call'd now a hen,
It had to be purifi'd then?
The reign of the Emperors is over,
What's the use of fighting for eating chicken however!
Babu says, "We wear *lungi* tucking behind our legs
Only to appease those shaven heads!"
Miah says, "We clipp'd the sign of Hinduism

In our cap to please your dogmatism!
In your *Baranoshi* live our so many brothers,
"When with rheumatic pain if one of us suffers.
We eat not rice anymore on the eleventh day of moon!"
Babu says, "We will start wearing *nagra* shoe instead of sandal soon!"
Miah says, "From the sin we're abstain'd for slaughtering cows as such!"
Babu says, " If you could have done that much,
Then give up eating that big one!"
Miah says, "Dada, anymore we eat not chicken,
Parata we cannot eat
Without meat!"

Babu says, " If you give up slaughtering cows,
Then after washing and smearing vermillion on it now
Let's take it to goddess's temple!"
Miah says, "In Allah's house if you utter not *Hari's* name humble,
An oxen I will let loose along with you,
Whatever will be the aftermath knows who!"

Suddenly there arous'd a big commotion,
As if 'tis a Hindu festival! With a bamboo in hand *Shombhu* ran,
Choku Miah took grapeshot in his hand!
Amidst hue and cry they start'd fighting,
Tikis and beards were flying,
In this way the two religions embrac'd
Each other by the virtue of the new pact!

Badna and *garu* have collid'd again!

Outcry came up there, ' Oh! The killings have begun!'
Towards mosque the *Miahs* scramble,
Hindu towards temple;
In the sky appear'd a question mark eternal,~
The piteous '*chandra bindu*' ~doleful!

A few words:

This song 'The Pact' was written by Poet satirically with some features to typify and describe the Muslims and Hindus in India. The song was written when the Muslims and Hindus in Bengal (India) were in communal riots on some politico-religious differences and disputes. A new pact was made to bring them into peace.

The badna and garu (the rioting Muslims and Hindus) embraced each other under the new pact.

The badna and garu are used by the Muslims and Hindus in two different names. Both badna and garu are small pitchers of water with a slender spout. Mentioning the badna and garu in the poem the Poet actually associated those two terms with the Muslims and Hindus in India. As he wrote ~'Badna and garu are in deep intimacy'.[Chandrabindu]

[16] The Reliance On The Graceful Feet

[Sohini- Ektala]

Why should we fear death as long as we've feet!
Brighten'd are miles ahead by the light
In the twinkling of an eye!
Subdu'd is the death; whole place is a refuge thereby,
Triumph to our reliance on the graceful feet!

Our boastful heads are abased? So our legs are long?
Showing everyone banana we walk ahead strong
From our childhood to the age of an old decrepit!
When police chases us to beat,
Instead of getting angry we step forward with our wise feet!

Chorus:
Why should we fear death as long as we've feet!
Brighten'd are miles ahead by the light
In the twinkling of an eye!
Subdu'd is the death; whole place is a refuge thereby,
Triumph to our reliance on the graceful feet!

Our body is like a bull frog, legs are like rubber,
O only when it is a necessity it moves over,
It moves to the places of garbage, in the bushes,
In jungles and ponds, near the ditches!
Gorges, woods, seas and mountains
It traverses,
In the same venue we're
The Hindus and Muslims united together!

Chorus:
Why should we fear death as long as we've feet!
Brighten'd are miles ahead by the light
In the twinkling of an eye!
Subdu'd is the death; whole place is a refuge thereby,
Triumph to our reliance on the graceful feet!
Everyone tells us, in the battle we retreat?
From behind someone makes quick exit?
I convulse with laughter!
When we move, we move forward thereafter,
We look not behind and around ever!
When we move ahead you call it a retreat, how?
Without further delay go to *Ranchi* now!

Chorus:
Why should we fear death as long as we've feet!
Brighten'd are miles ahead by the light
In the twinkling of an eye!
Subdu'd is the death; whole place is a refuge thereby,
Triumph to our reliance on the graceful feet!

Death will be exhaust'd for running after us,
Death angel too will be breathless,
Then on its left leg life stands!
Once upon a time in the same god's
Lineage we had been –our feet still bear that memory!
When we move, we fly in the sky,
Our *dhooti* too drops off and flies!

Chorus:
Why should we fear death as long as we've feet!
Brighten'd are miles ahead by the light

In the twinkling of an eye!
Subdu'd is the death; whole place is a refuge thereby,
Triumph to our reliance on the graceful feet!
This is the path shown by our fathers and grandfathers
And follow'd by many distinguish'd others!
As stated by some saintly persons god will be found
In this path on any day next !
If you die, then you truly died!
And the one who escap'd,
By dint of his feet he was sav'd!

Chorus:
Why should we fear death as long as we've feet!
Brighten'd are miles ahead by the light
In the twinkling of an eye!
Subdu'd is the death; whole place is a refuge thereby,
Triumph to our reliance on the graceful feet!
[Chandrabindu]

A few words:
It is a satirical chorus song. Here poet criticizes the people of the country who are timid and do not want to sacrifice their life. When country needed an uprising the people ran away and were scared of death. They ran headlong without looking back. Why should they fear death when they have graceful feet to flee away?

[17] Wash The Body Of The Cow

Chorus : Wash the body of the cow !!
Everything is turn'd upside down— the rule of destiny, ritual,
Religion, nation and justice perpetual!
Women fight with each other,
While men enjoy a picnic together!
Father runs away with tickets
While His daughter starts
Picketing! Wife turns the wheel of handloom now,
Husband squanders time washing the cow!

Chorus : Wash the body of the cow !!

Cobblers and sweepers do better in calling
Strikes, Police tests the thickness of our skin!
Chaterjees keep beard,
In barber's house *Miah* goes to shave beard!
'Touch me not!'- That bad smell'd weird *Bhuzpuri*-
Scream'd at *Bangali!*

Chorus : Wash the body of the cow !!

Tying *paita* around their waist the Brahmins
Can cook for anybody within means!
If they're touch'd, they mind not,
If their home's touch'd, throw they utensils out!
In the meetings of heathens there
Go the girls, men say "O God, let's cut and run from here!"
Vegetable and gruel of rice when the boys eat,
Seeing them eating the elders get
Sweaty and thus retreat!

Chorus : Wash the body of the cow !!

Out of fear, *Miah* puts not his cap on the head,
A *Gopal-kacha* he wears instead,
Hindus put Gandhi-cap, uncles wear *Lunghi* piece!
Behind the bamboo trees they hide seeing police!
The bat-nosed *Roy-bahadur, Khan-bahadur*
He becomes losing his ear!

Chorus : Wash the body of the cow !!

Troubles he creates the war-monger leader,
Country can not go on like that for-ever!
'Anointing my oil on head boldness can be Cured'–
Says the bold-headed,
Says the deaf, 'What a song he sings'–
The blind says, 'What a dance she performs!'
The hunch-back says, 'help me to sleep,
To lie down what a relief!'

Chorus : Wash the body of the cow !!

There comes the hackneyed cheaper *Swaraj*,
Burnt egg-plant the virtuous eats,
The worthless rides horse and cars,
Putting his leg on the back of a frog
The lame ridicules at another crippl'd hog!

Chorus : Wash the body of the cow !!!
[Chandrabindu]
A few words:
In the poem the poet narrated satirically the socio-political

situation that existed in the society of Hindus and Muslims in Bengal, India. He criticized the ignorant people of the society who seemed to be very much attached with their own culture and belief though they socialize with each other for the sake of socialization.

Omar Khayyam Geeti

[18] In A Dawn Of Creation
(Shindhu-kafi-kawalee)

O Lord, in a dawn of creation when Thou hadst creat'd me,
My destiny Thou hadst known, my life~ how it would be!
O Lord, by Thee 'twas decreed,
If ever sin we commit about
The dread of hell Thou dost
Warn us, we've to to abide by Thy judgement!

O the Merciful, for the sake of mercy
If Thou showest us mercy,
Then why from the heaven Adam Thou hadst
Cast out for the mistake he made!
Always by Thy mercy savest Thou the devoted one,
But that mercy from Thee he has earn'd,
O Lord, embrace the ungodly,
Merciful he will call thee!
[Nazrul Geetika]

[19] O the Young Lover
(Bhairab-kawalee)

O the young lover! Let the heartless
Lover know thy pain of love, O the victorious!
Captivate her whole heart with thine
Illusory image charming!
Equal not are thousands
Of *Ka'aba* and mosques
To one heart, look not
For *ka'aba,* in the shadow of heart
Look for thine intention, the light
Of love that illuminates the heart
Spreads equally over the temple, mosque,
Church and synagogue!

In the book of love he will persist ever,
Glowfully will be written his name there,
For hell he has no fear,
For heaven he keeps no desire!
[Nazrul Geetika]

A few words:

Those two poems of Omar Khayyam were translated by poet Kazi Nazrul Islam into Bengali. I tried my utmost to adhere the spirit of Khayyam's originality that Poet Nazrul kept in his translation. As we know Syed Mujtaba Ali wrote: "the translation of Kazi is the Kazi of all translations."

The great Persian Sufi Poet (1048–1131) Khayyam's mystic philosophy is reflected on those two poems. It is about the Lord, the

God of universe, His power, His love and mercy and His light of love that illuminates our heart.

GLOSSARY

Agastya: A Hindu mythological sage of India.

Agomoni: An arrival song or any song about the coming of Uma (Shiva's wife) to her father's house as told in the Mahabharata (Hindu myth).

Ahallya: Wife of the sage Gautama, primarily known for her sexual encounter with the god-king Indra. She was cursed by her husband but subsequently she was liberated by god Vishnu [Hindu myth].

Akbar : (14 October 1542 – 27 October 1605) He is known as the Akbar the Great. He was Mughal Emperor from 1556 until his death. He was the third and greatest ruler of the Mughal Dynasty in India.

Aman: Winter paddy of Bangladesh.

Ameer: The King.

Ampara : The suras of the 30th or the last part of the holy Qur'an.

Amrita: The heavenly invigorating drink or nectar.

Anchal: The marginal part or the end part of a strip of long unstitched cloth (sari) hangs loosely at the back and over the shoulder. The sari is worn by Bangladeshi and Indian women.

Andaman Island: There are some Islands that form an archipelago in the Bay of Bengal between India to the west and Myanmar to the north and east. In 1789, the British colonial government in India established a naval base and a penal colony in Andaman Island to use it as a settlement to punish mostly political prisoners of main land India. Thus the colonial ruler used to separate them from the general populace by placing them in the remote location.

Most part of the Andaman and Nicobar Islands are under the Union Territory of India, while a small number in the north of the archipelago, including the Coco Islands, belong to Myanmar.

Arafat: It a sacred valley in Makkah between mountains, the Hajj pilgrimage gather there to offer prayers.

Arash : The meaning of the Arabic word 'Arash' is chair or throne. The seating place (the throne) of King of the heavens and earth, Allah (swt) or the God.

Aroti: Waving lamps or candles infront of the Hindu deities. The ritual is observed by the Hindu.

Arjuna : He was an ambidextrous archer. He was the third of the five Pandava brothers and the third son of Pandu. Krishna and Arjuna fought the battle of Kurukshetra to defeat Kauravas. He was considered to be the hero of the Hindu epic *Mahabharata*. (Hindu myth)

Ari chacha : Ari(concealment, hiding) Chacha (uncle) : A slang word for a Muslim who conceals his identity in public. The word is used usually in West Bengal, India.

Ashar: A hot summer monsoon month of Bangla calendar year.

Ashabori: An Indian classical mode of music.

As-salam: It is a greeting saying peace upon you. Muslim greets each other saying As-salam or As salamu alaikum.

Ashwin: The 6th month of Bangla calendar year. The end of monsoon in Bangladesh.

Ashok : Its botanical name is *Saraca asoca*. It grows in the eastern Himalaya and other parts of India and Bangladesh. Ashoka is a small evergreen tree with paripinnate leaves.

Astha or Ashta-dikpal: (Myth): The King of the horizon where the setting of the sun and moon takes place.

Ashur : A demon (Hindu myth).

Atar: A kind of fragrance derived from the oil of agar or eucalyptus plants.

Aurongazeb : (4 November 1618 - 3 March 1707) He was the sixth Mughal Emperor and ruled over most of the Indian subcontinent. His reign lasted for 49 years from 1658 until his death in 1707.

Azrael : The angel of death.

Babla : Its botanical name is *Acacia nilotica*. It is a small to medium sized ever-green tree with golden-yellow flowers, fragrant and crowded in long-stalked heads.

Babu: A respectful appellation is used to address a Hindu gentleman. It can be affixed to the name of a Hindu (Like Mr.).

Babus: It is the plural number of Babu. Babu is the name of a boy. Here '*pond of the Babus*' means the palm-pond belongs to all members of babu's family i.e., to babu's parents, brothers and sisters.

Badna: A kind of small pitcher with a slender spout (it is usually used by the Muslims in Indian sub-continent).

Bajrapani: (Hindu myth) : The thunderer, Indra, the god of thunder and clouds.

Balaram or Balarama:: He is half brother of Krishna who carries a plough on his shoulder.(Hindu myth)

Bangla: The undivided Bengal (East and West Bengal) of India (before the year 1947). Bangla is also a language of the people of Bangladesh and West Bengal, India.

Bangali : The people of Bangladesh and bangla speaking people of Assam and West Bengal, India.

Bani: Goddess Shwaraswati is also known as Bani. she is also goddess of speech (Hindu myth).

Baranoshi: A name of the city in India.

Baroan: An Indian mode (raga) of classical music.

Bashanta: One of the six seasons in Bangladesh. The flower-blooming season. The Spring in Bangladesh.

Bashudeva : Father of Lord Krishna (Hindu Myth).

Baul: Wandering minstrel or a group of wandering minstrels in Bangladesh.

Behala (violin): A stringed musical instrument. It is usually with four strings. It is one of the smallest and highest-pitched string instruments.

Bel or Beli : A kind of sweet-smelling flower, the Arabian Jasmine, *Jasminum Sambac*.

Beday: They are the nomadic ethnic group in Bangladesh. They lead a life like gypsy. They move from place to place usually by boat and earn their livelihood by snake charming, snake catching and selling, etc.

Bhatiyali: A musical mode sung by the boatmen of Bangladesh.

Bhaishak : It is the first month of Bangla calendar year. The month of storm and rain.

Behag raga : It is a raga or mode of Indian classical music.

Bhagiroti: The river Ganges begins at the confluence of the

Bhagirathi and Alaknanda rivers. The Bhagirathi rises at the foot of Gangotri Glacier, at Gaumukh, at an elevation of 3,892 m (12,769 ft).

Bhaishaki : Pertaining to the month of Bhaishak.

Bhairab: A manifestation of Shiva (Hindu myth). It is also an Indian musical mode.

Bhairabi: A famale ascetic who worships Hindu god Shiva (Hindu myth).

Bhairabi : An Indian musical mode.

Bharoti : Saraswati- the goddess of speech (Hindu myth).

Bhatiali : A Bengali folk musical mode.The boatmen of downstream area of Bangladesh sing their songs in this musical mode with a stoic melody.

Bhojpuri : The people of Bhojpur, north-eastern part of India.

Bholanath: Another name of Lord Shiva(Hindu myth.)

Bhisma: The 8th son goddess Ganga and king Santanu according to Mahabaharata [Hindu myth].

Bhrigu : One of the seven sages, a warrior sage (Hindu myth).

Bhuzpuris : The people of Bhujpur, India.

Bihaga: An Indian Classical raga(mode) of music.

Bina or Vina: This musical instrument is about 4 feet (1.2 metres) in length. It has two resonating gourds under each end of its hollow wooden body. It has 24 high movable frets, and four metal melody strings and three metal drone strings running along the length of the body(according to Encyclopaedia Britanica).

Binapani : One who holds a vina in one's hand; Goddess Saraswati (Hindu myth).

Bindhyacal/Vindhyachal: The Vindhyachal Mountain is in Chhattisgarh, UP, India.

Bokul: Yellowish white flowers with sweet smell. Its latin name is *Mimusops elengi*.

Borrak: According to Muslim-belief Prophet Mohammad (pbuh) was carried by this horse-like creature to ascend the heavens to meet Allah (swt).

Borun: The God of Sea (Hindu myth).

Bose: A Hindu family title.

Braja : A village near Mathura where Krishna passed his childhood (Hindu myth).

Brahma: He is the Hindu god (deva) of creation and one of the Trimurtis [Hindu myth].

Bhrigu: One of the seven sages(Saptarishis); a warrior sage. He was the first compiler of predictive astrology, and also the author of Bhrigu Samhita, the astrological (Jyotish) classic written during the Vedic period. He also tested the divine power of three deities- Brahma, Shiva and Vishnu(Hindu myth).

Brindaban: A city of Uttarpradesh, India. It is considered to be a place where Lord Krishna spent his early childhood [Hindu myth].

Buddha: (563 to 460 BC). He was a great Buddhist saint. His name is Siddartha Gautama Buddha. He was the founder of Buddhism

Bulbuli : Family: Pycnonotidae. The Genus: *Pycnonotus*.

Bulbuls are medium-sized songbirds and indigenous to Bangladesh. Some are with yellow, red or orange vents in cheek and throat. Some species have distinct crests.

Byomkesh : A name of Shiva. Byomkesh constitutes two parts-*byom* (sky or air) and *kesh* (hair). He stood high, behind him was the sky. He was holding the river Ganges in his matted hair and allowed the holy river to traverse the earth (Hindu myth).

*Chaiti: The word chaiti is related to the features or characteristics of the month of chaitra— the last month of Bangla calendar year.

Chandal: Someone who deals with disposal of corpses in the crematorium. They are untouchables. They belong to the lower caste in Hindu society.

Chandan: Also known as sandalwood.

Chakra: A spinning wheel used as a weapon by Lord Vishnu(Hindu myth).

Chamily or Chameli: Spanish jasmine : *Jasminum grandiflorum* . It is a sweet-smelling white flower.

Chandra bindu: One of the Bangla alphabetical signs to pronounce any word created from nasal part. It looks like a crescent moon with a dot in the center.

Chapa: Also known as champa or golden champa : *Michelia champaca* . It is indigenous to Bangladesh. It is a large evergreen tree with 18-21 m in height. The flowers are with few yellowish white petals with sweet smell.

Char: A strip of sandy land rises from the bed of river or sea above the water-level. The char forms by the deposition of silt.

Chaterjees : The title for the respectable(Brahmin) Hindus.

Chayanaut: A serene Indian musical mode(raga).

Chandi: Goddess of power- combination of Durga, Lakshmi, and Saraswati (Hindu myth).

Charka: It means wheel ; people make threads by spinning the wheel with hand. In this poem the Poet mentioned particularly about the wheel of handloom of Mahatma Gandhi. He started this hanloom movement against the British ruler in India. Under the guidance of Gandhi, charkha and Indian handloom products gained back their glory.

Choka: They are small to medium-large freshwater diving birds, known as grebes. They have lobed toes, and are excellent swimmers and divers. However, they have their feet placed far back on the body, making them quite ungainly on land. There are 20 species worldwide and 2 species which occur in Bangladesh.

Choka-choki: The terms are the masculine and feminine gender of the bird Choka.

Chokor: Latin name: *Caccabis chucar*- a game bird in the pheasant family. This partridge has its native range in Asia from Israel and Turkey through Afghanistan to India, along the inner ranges of the Western Himalayas to Nepal. This bird flies upward in the sky during the moon-lit night.

Chokori: The feminine gender of Chokor

Choku Miah: A name of a Muslim male.

Chordi: In Hindu Bangali family the younger sister is addressed as Chordi. Chordi is from 'choto didi'. Choto means little or younger, didi means sister.

Clive : Robert Clive(29 September 1725 - 22 November 1774), also known as Clive of India, was a British officer who established the military and political supremacy of the East India Company in Bengal , India.

Conch: It is a spiral mollusk shell, usually used to produce sound by blowing air from the mouth through spiral shell.

Cooli: A class of people in Indian subcontinent who work in railway stations to carry luggages of the passengers. The workers in the tea gardens in India and Bangladesh are known also as cooli.

Crore: A unit of value equal to ten million or100 lakhs. Origin:Hindi & Urdu *karor*.

Dada: This is the term usually used to address a Hindu gentleman as one's brother.

Dadhial: A small bird like magpie robin in Bangladesh.

Dahuk: A kind of water bird in Bangladesh.They live in low and marshy lands around jheels and haors of Bangladesh.

Dajjal: One-eyed man.

Dala : A big flattened plate or tray, made of cane, bamboo or metal to carry fruits and flowers.

Datura: The thorn apple. Its botanical name: *Datura stramonium.* Datura species are herbaceous, leafy and short-lived perennials. It contains a kind of alkaloid that affects the nervous system to cause delirium.

Datakarna : A person of boundless generosity (Hindu myth).

Dayamanti : Damayanti was a princess of Vidarbha Kingdom. She was of such beauty and grace that even the gods could not stop from admiring her (Hindu myth.)

Deayali: or Diwali : A Hindu festival, involves the lighting of small clay lamps filled with oil to signify the triumph of good over evil.

deng-deng : The words have no particular meaning but are expressed when someone dances out of fun in a rhythmless way.

Derhem: Arabian coin Dirham

Dewani-Aam: -It was a palace built like a hall for the public so that they could gather there and talk to the Emperor about their problems during the Mughal period in India.

Dharmaraj: He was a king in Hindu epic Mahabharata. *Dharmaraj*, meaning the 'righteous king'; for his piety he was known as Yudhisthira (Hindu myth).

Dheki: A kind of wooden husking pedal operated by village wives in a see-saw manner by pressing it with their feet.

Dhonuja-duloni: The another name of the goddess Durga (Hindu myth).

Dhooti : A piece of unstiched cloth worn by the Hindus by tucking between the legs at the waistband.

Dhiraj : An ancient king of India. (Hindu mythology).

Dhup: A kind of dry resin collected from certain kind of plants used for fume after kindling fire on it.

Dhurjati: The name of god Shiva(Hindu myth).

Digbalika: An imaginary virgin girl who is one of the ten quarters of the sky or horizon. *Dig* means any direction or any one of the ten quarters of the horizon; *balika* means girl.

Dilruba: The dilruba is a stringed musical instrument

played with a bow. It is made of wood and animal skin.

Dil-afruz: The one who awakens the heart.

Durbasha: A mythological saint notorious for his quick temper and harsh words (Hindu Myth).

Duhshasana: He was the second son of the blind King Dhritarashtra and Gandhari in the epic Mahabharata, and the younger brother of Duryodhana. (Hindu myth)

Duldul: A name of a horse ridden by hazarat Imam Hussain.

Duryodhana: He is the eldest son of the blind king Dhritarashtra and Queen Gandhari, the eldest of the one hundred Kaurava brothers. (Hindu myth)

Dodhichi: He was a votary of Shiva. As per legend in Mahabharata, it is said that thunderbolt of Indra was formed from the bones of Dadhichi. The gods used his bones to make weapons to defeat the Asur. (Hindu myth)

Dolon chapa: Commonly known as the butterfly lily in English.

In Bangla we call it Dolon Chapa. Its botanical name is *Hedychium coronarium*.

Dolon chapa occupies significant area in our literature.

Durbasha: A mythological saint notorious for his quick temper and harsh words

(Hindu myth).

Eid: A religious festival of Muslim.

Eidgah: it is a place where prayer takes place in a big congregation during the Eid day; usually it is a big field with cemented floor surrounded by wall.

Eid-ul-fitr: This is one of the two religious festivals of Muslim. This is the day after completion of thirty days of fasting in Ramadan.

Eid mubarok: Eid Mubarok means "Blessed Festival". It's a way of saying "Eid Mubarok" at the time of the Islamic Eid holidays.

Fagun: or falgun – It is the eleventh month of the Bangla calendar year. It is the month of the spring season in Bangladesh.

Kama: Hindu god of love(Hindu Myth).

Falguni: Referring to the eleventh month of Bangla calendar month Falgun.

Farhad: A character in Arabian story famous for his love. He sacrificed his life for his lover Shiri.

Farhad-Shiri; Laili- Majnu: Legendary characters from the stories of Arabian literature.

They were lovers. They loved each other and sacrificed them in loving each other. Farhad loved Shiri and Majnu loved Laili.

Fateha: Al- Fateha, the first verse in the Noble Quran.

Fathima: The daughter of Prophet Muhammad (pbuh).

Ferry-Ghat: The landing-stage on the banks of a river where people gather to cross the river from both sides by a boat.

Firnee: A kind of food made of rice, milk and sugar or molasses

Furat : The river Euphrates.

Ghat: A landing stage on the bank of river or ponds or lakes built for for bathing or fetching water.

Gajon: A festival of worshipping Shiva in the month of chaitra.(Hindu religious festival) (According to Sailendra Biswas's Samsad Bengali to English dictionary).

Ganga: The goddess and consort of Shiva [Hindu myth].

Garu : A small pitcher or a tankard with a spout(it is usually used by the Hindus of India.)

Gazni Mahmud: Mahmud was born in 971 AD in the town of Gazni in Medieval Khorasan(what is now south-eastern Afghanistan).He reigned from 2 October 971 - 30 April 1030. He was the most prominent ruler of the Ghaznavid Empire in India.

Gandiba: (Hindu myth.): It is the name of Arjuna's bow (Hindu myth).

Gangotri: One of the glaciers of the Himalayas, the origin of the river Ganges, it is also a town and seat of goddess Ganga at Uttarakand, India.

Garo: The Garos are a tribal people in Meghalaya, India and neighboring areas of Bangladesh.

Gazal: An extraordinary song with variety of expression around its central themes of love and separation. Most of the ghazals are now sung in various styles and not limited to khayal, thumri and raga. Gazals are written mainly in the form of sher or poetry in Urdu.

Geeta: Geeta is a Hindu scripture with verses and a part of the ancient sanskrit epic, the Mahabharata.

Gini-pagal': A name of a variety of fine rice in India.

Girijaya: She is a wife of Shiva. She is also known as Parboti (Hindu Myth).

Golapjam: Rose Apples. Latin name :*Syzygium jambos*. One of the popular fruits in Bangladesh.

Gokul: Another name of Krishna(Hindu mythology) *Gokul Nag: Lord Krishna was named as Gokulnag. It is described in the Holy Gita that he killed a poisonous snake,Kalia Nag (cobra) from a big lake while he was a baby.He stayed in Gokul, *the* legendary 'cow-village' in Northern India during his childhood (Hindu myth).

Gomoti: A river in India. The Hindu considers the river as sacred.

Gopal: The name of lord Krishna. (Hindu Myth).

Gopal-kacha: A loin-cloth (dhuti) worn by the Hindus by tucking behind between the legs at the waistband.

Gori : An unmarried, fair- complexioned young girl.

Gorur : A sacred bird of god Vishnu with pointed beak. Vishnu rides on its back. (Hindu myth). Hindu worship Gorur as a deity.

Granth sahib: The holy scripture of the Sikhs, regarded as the teachings of the Ten Gurus. It is the source or guide of prayer for the Sikhs and pivotal in Sikh worship.

Gritachi: An Apsara or celestial nymph. She had amours with many great sages and mortal men.

Gul bagicha : (origin: Persian word) Gul means flower, bagicha means garden; the flower garden.

Gul bakauli: The queen of the angels mentioned in Arabian story.

Gul rukh: It means rose-faced. Persian words 'Gul' means rose and 'rukh' means face

Gur-muri: Gur means molasses; Muri means a kind of cereal made by parching rice on hot sand.

Habia Dozak: The seventh hell- the hell with intensely hot fire in its abyss.This is the most terrible hell among all other hells created by God.

Habus: (*Habus* is the plural number of Habu). Habu is a name of a boy. Here *'greyhound of the habus'* means the greyhound belongs to the family of habu i.e., to his parents, brothers and sisters.

Hambira: An Indian meditative musical mode(raga).

Haram: The word means forbidden or unlawful--anything that is forbidden by God for the mankind.

Hari The name of a Hindu deity.

Harischandra: He is the 36th king of the Solar Dynasty(Hindu Myth).

Haruth, Maruth: They are two angels. In Islamic theology angels do not possess free will and cannot commit sin. Once angels became astonished at the acts of disobedience committed by the human beings on earth.Harut and Marut were selected by God and sent to the earth with human attribution. Harut and Marut eventually succumbed to their human lusts and fell into all sins.

Hasnahena: The creamy white flowers clustered in a stalk spread sweet fragrance all around when they bloom in the night. Its botanical name: *Cestrum nocturnum*. It grows in Bangladesh and India.

Hassan, Hussain : They are two grandsons of Prophet Mohammed(pbuh). They are sons of Ali and Fatima.

Hafez: A famous Persian Poet (1325-1390)

Hashantika : A vessel for holding fire, a fire-pot, a fire-urn.

Hem : Another name of Uma or Parvati, the wife of Shiva (Hindu myth).

Hemanta: It comprises two months—Kartik and Agrahayan of Bangla calendar year. It precedes the season '*Sheet*' or winter in Bangladesh.

Herem: Harem was a palace or a building where concubines and slave girls were confined for the pleasure of the Mughal emperors. The harems accommodated a large number of women from different races and communities in India and Persia.

Hindol: The raga emerges from Kalyan thaat. It is an ancient raga associated with the spring season. It is a raga of four swaras (tones of the scale).

Indrani: Wife and consort of Indra- the god of wars, thunder storm, and rainfall (Hindu myth).

Hizal: Indian oak, *Barringotonia acutangula*. The plant grows in abundance in Bangladesh and India.

Indra : The king of all gods, the lord of thunder and lightning (Hindu myth).

Israfil: The angel who will blow the trumpet twice on the Day of Judgment (the doomsday).

Joban: In India some Hindus consider the Muslims in India as joban, the foreigners who came from the foreign lands.

Jamadagni: One of the seven great sages (Saptarishis) and the father of Parashurama, the sixth incarnation of Vishnu (Hindu myth).

Jhamjham : A pattering sound of heavy rainfall when the

rain drops on the leaves, roofs and water surface of the surroundings.

Jakkha/ Jaksa: A demon who guards the treasure of Kuvera, the king of Jakkhas

(Hindu Myth).

Jaksapuri: (Hindu myth) : The city of Jaksa- the demons who protect the treasure of king Kuvera..

Jhamrul: A kind of fruit known as Wax Jambu, Latin name: *Syzygium samarangense*. It is one of the popular fruits in Bangladesh.

Jamuna : A name of a river in India.

Janoki : The daughter of king Janoka (Hindu myth).

Jari : A kind of folk-song of Bengal (composed in memory of the martyrs at Karbala and sung usually in Bangladesh on the occasion of Muharram, a holy month.)

Jhat : The people inhabit Sindh, Punjab, Haryana, Uttar Pradesh and Rajasthan. They took arms against the Mughal Empire during the late 17th and early 18th centuries.

Joshuda/ Jashuda : The foster mother of Lord Krishna (Hindu myth).

Judhistir : The name of the eldest son of King Pandu (Hindu myth).

Jui : Jasmine flower, *Jasmine sambac*; the small shrub plant bears white colored flowers with sweet smell.

Juthi: A kind of jasmine flower with sweet smell.

Ka'aba: The sacred house of God in Makkah. It is the holiest house for the Muslim. The Muslims pray facing towards the Ka'aba five times a day.

Kadam/ Kadamba: A large tree (about 148ft in height) that bears flowers in the rainy seaon. The flowers are sweetly fragrant, sepals are orange in colour; bristles of cream-white petals are in clusters with terminal globular heads spread out from a round ball. The entire flower looks like a round cushion with pins all around it. Its botanical name is *Nauclea cadamba*.

kafer: Unbelievers.

Kailash : A name of a city in northern India at the foot of the mountain Himalaya.

Kajla: Pertaining to black complexion.

Kalidaha: it is a deep river or lake- an abode of serpents and lotus. This lake was visited by sages to make their wishes [Hindu myth].

Kalmi: A kind water creeper plant. Latin name: *Ipomoea aquatica*.

Kalpurusha: (Indian myth.) He is an envoy of Yama- the god of death. Kalpurush was a handsome hunter and in human form he is a destroyer. He is like the Orion of Greek mythology.

Kama: He is the god of love and desire. Kama literally means trishna(Sanskrit) i.e. desire or thirst (Hindu myth).

Kamini: Its common name is orange Jasmine. Botanical name: *Murraya paniculata*. Kamini flowers have orange-like fragrance. Tree are small to medium in height.

Kalopahar: A Hindu Brahmin who after embracing Islam turned into an iconoclast; a decrier of current Hindu beliefs in worshipping idols.

Kamranga: Latin name: *Averrhoa corumbola*. It is one of the popular fruits in Bangladesh.

Kama:(Hindu Myth.) The Hindu god of love or desire.

Kamsa : He is the brother of Devaki, and ruler of the Vrishni kingdom with its capital at Mathura .He was killed by Krishna (Hindu Myth).

Karbala : A town in Iraq where a battle took place on Muharram 10, and on October 10, 680 AD. The battle was between a small group of supporters of Prophet Muhammad (pbuh)'s grandson Husain ibn Ali, and a much larger military detachment from the forces of Yazid, the Umayyad Caliph.

Kashi: The Kashi is a city located in Varanasi in the state of Uttar Pradesh, India.

Khaled: He was also known as Khalid-ibn-Walid (592–642). He was a companion of Prophet Muhammad (pbuh). He was noted for his military tactics and prowess.

Khan-bahadur: The title was offered to the respectable Muslims by the British government in India.

Khatun-e Jannath: 'The woman of paradise'. The word 'khatun' means woman, 'Jannath' means paradise. Fathima, the daughter of Prophet Muhammaed (pbuh) was honored by this title.

Keshob: Name of Lord Krishna(Hindu Myth).

Koohinur: The name of a precious diamond embedded in the Pea cock throne of Mughal Emperor Shahjahan.

Kori : A kind of small shells.

Krishna: An incarnation of lord Vishnu in Hindu Vagavata Purana myths. Krishna is often described as an infant or young boy playing a flute as in the Bhagavata Purana, He was portrayed as a god-child, a divine hero and the supreme being (Hindu myth).

Krishna: Hindu deity Lord Krishna blew a conch (panchajanya) in the battle of Kurukshetra ((Hindu myth).

Krishna Dvaipayana : He is the author as well as a character in the Mahabharata and considered to be the scribe of both the Vedas, and the supplementary texts such as the Puranas[Hindu myth].

Kufa: A name of a city in Iraq.

Kurukshetra: In the epic of Mahabharata a battle took place in the field of kurukshetra between two families- Pandavas and Kauravas for kingship. (Hindu myth)

Kuru: According to the Indian epic poem Mahabharata, a dynastic succession struggle took place between two groups of cousins(the Kauravas and Pandavas) of an Indo-Aryan kingdom called Kuru for the throne of Hastinapura. (Hindu myth)

Kupo-munduk : A narrow-minded person with limited knowledge or vision.

Laili: The legendary character, famous for her love and dedication to her beloved Majnu.

Lanka: In old Hindu mythology the Lanka, the present day Srilanka was burnt in a battle between Rama and Ravana. The city Lanka was burnt (Hindu myth).

LankaKando: The war took place to capture Lanka by Ram as per epic in Hindu Ramayana. It is the battle in Lanka between the monkeys and the demon armies of Ravana. After Ravana is defeated, Sita undergoes the test of fire, completes exile with Rama, and they return to Ayodhya to reign over the Ideal State. (Hindu myth)

Laskmi: The Hindu goddess of wealth and prosperity. She is the consort of Lord Vishnu[Hindu myth].

Lat-Manat: The two female goddesses. They were worshipped as deities by ancient Arab pagans in pre-Islamic period.

Lova-Kusha: The twin sons of Rama and Shita[Hindu myth].

Luffa: In Bangladesh the local name of Luffa is Jhinga. It is a vegetative plant under the Family Cucurbitaceae. It is commonly known as ridged gourd. (see the note)

Lunghi/ Lungi: A piece of stitched cloth worn mainly by the Muslims in eastern India and Bangladesh.

Mahabali: He was a king of the Asuras. He brought entire world under his benevolent rule – and was even able to conquer the underworld and Heaven, which he wrested from Indra and the Devas. (Hindu Myth)

Mehdi: His coming is prophesied. He will stay on Earth for seven, nine or nineteen years (according to various interpretations) before the Day of Judgment to salvage the world of wrongdoing, injustice and tyranny.

Miah: It is an appellation of courtesy affixed to the name of a Muslim gentleman (like Mr.).

Madan: The god of love in Hindu myths. He carries always bow and arrow to shoot the arrow of love (Hindu myth).

Mandir: Hindu's temple for worshiping.

Mathura: Mathura is the birthplace of Lord Krishna at the

centre of Braj or Brij-bhoomi in Uttar Pradesh, India.

Mejo/Mejla: Second-born; second in order of seniority among brothers, or sisters, or uncles, or aunts, or in-laws.

Miah: It is an appellation of courtesy affixed to the name of a Muslim gentleman (like Mr.)

Miah bhai: It is also an appellation of courtesy affixed to the name of a Muslim gentleman to address him more respectfully.

Moinamoti sari: A trade name of a sari in Bangladesh. Sari is usually designed and beautified with prints and colors. There are different types and qualities of sari. Sari is worn by the women of Indian subcontinent. Its length ranges from five to six yards.

Mohua: Latin name: *Madhuca longifolia*. The flowers are fleshy, off white in color, and emit attractive sweet fragrance when the plant is in full bloom. It is indigenous to Bangladesh and India.

Momtaj: She was wife of Mughal Emperor Shah Jahan. Her name prior to marriage was Arjumand Banu Begum (April 1593- June 1631). Mumtaj had deep and loving marriage with Shahjahan. The Tajmohal, her final burial place was named from her name Mumotaj.

Molla: A Muslim cleric.

Mollika(also Beli): The flower is white with pleasant fragrance. Its botanical name: *Jasminum sambac*.

Momotaj: She was an Empress and wife of ShahJahan (The Mughal Emperor in India from 1628 to 1658).

Mumtaj Mahal/ *Mumtaj*: The wife of Mughal Emperor, Shahjahan (1628-1658), in India.

Mongal: In Indian Vedic Astrology Mongal(Mars) is considered to be one of the twenty seven stars. The Hindu worships the star as deity.

Moral: They are the water-birds of Bangladesh live in the vast low lying areas of the country.

Morshia: It is the recitation or singing song from the traditional folk-poetry about the tragedy of karbala battle in front of large audiences.

Muharram : The first month of the Islamic(Arabic) calendar year. An annual celebration takes place in this month commemorating the death of Hussain, grandson of Prophet Muhammad (pbuh).

Mujra: Mujra is a form of dance originated during Mughal era performed by female dancers.It is a mixture of an art and exotic dance.

Munna: This is a name of a slave girl mentioned in the poem.

Mushaira : An evening social gathering where poetry is read.

Saki: A young female attendant who serves wine.

Nag: A Hindu deity in the form of snake (King Cobra) (Hindu Myth).

Nagini: A sanskrit word for a Hindu deity who can take a form of the snake (King Cobra). Nagini is the feminine gender of Nag.*Narayan*: Narayana is the name of the Supreme god in his infinite all pervading form. He is also known as Vishnu. (Hindu myth)

Nagra: A kind of shoes flat and bent little bit upward at the tip usually worn by the Muslim in Bangladesh, Pakistan and India.

Nari kacha: A piece of cloth(dhuti) which is tucked by the wearer between the legs at the waistband.

Nawab: 'Nawab' means 'governor of the region'. They were appointed by the Mughal Emperors during their reign in India. It is also a title awarded as a personal distinction for various services to the Government of Brtish India.

Nilachal: It is believed to be an abode of Hindu deity Jagannath. It is in Puri, India. It is a place of high religious significance in Hinduism.

Nilkantha: The Lord Shiva who swallowed a sea of poison and kept it in his throat that turned into blue. (Hindhu myth).). 'Nil' means blue and 'kantha' means throat.

Nimai : An ascetic mendicant .

Non-violent movement: Mohandas K. Gandhi organized the non-violent and the non- cooperation movement against the British colonial government in India in 1920. The Non Cooperation Movement and the role played by Gandhi took the Indian freedom movement to new heights. It ushered in a new political fervor among the Indian people.

Noroj: Persian new year's day.

Nrisinha : Means the Man-lion.The fourth incarnation of Vishnu in the form of a being whose upper half of the body was like a man whilst the lower half was like a lion. (Hindu myth)

Notobor: The chief dancer.Also it is the name of Sri Krishna (Hindu Mythology).

Nupur: An anklet set with small bells used by dancers(man and woman) to make rhythmic beating steps with tabla and also to display as an ornament attached around their ankles.

Nurjahan: The wife of Mughal Emperor Jehanghir (1577-1645) in India.

* *Oghran* same as *Agrahayana*: The eighth month of the Bangla calendar year. It precedes the winter month.

Oloka: The kingdom of Kuvera, the kingdom full of wealth and immence fortune.

(Hindu Myth).

Omar: Omar Khayyam, a famous Persian Poet (1048-1131).

Oparajita: A bluish flower of a creeper plant. Its botanical name is *Clitoria ternatea*. The plant grows in moist, neutral soil. The deep blue flowers are with light yellow markings.

Orjun: He was a skilled archer, played a key role to defeat the Kauravas in the Kurukshetra war (Hindu myth).

Orpheus: Orpheus was the greatest musician, flutist and poet (Greek myth).

Pai: An obsolete Indian coin(1 rupee=16 anas=192 pai).

Paita: A kind of sacred threads worn by the people of superior Hindu castes (Brahmin).

Pandavas: In Mahabharata epic Pandavas are five brothers-five sons of King Pandu. (Hindu myth)

Pancajanya: The conch was blown by Krishna in the battle of kurukshetra. (Hindu myth)

Papiya: An indigenous bird in Bangladesh renowned for its sweet note. It is also known as Indian cuckoo.

Papiya- Shayma: In Bangladesh the pied cuckoo is known as

Papiya. Latin name: *Clamator jacobinus*. Shayma and papiya both are cuckoos and indigenous to Bangladesh.

Parata : It is a kind of hand made flour bread and fried with butter oil or regular edible oil.

Parijat: Coral tree; botanical name: *Erythrina indica*, also one of the five trees of heaven((Hindu Myth).

Parsurama: A warrior ovotar of lord Vishnu who carries an axe. He was the sixth incarnation of lord Vishnu. He was the youngest son of Jamadagni. He was ever-obedient and righteous.

Parul and *Sat Bhai Champa:* 'Parul' and 'Sat bhai champa' are the characters of one of the fairy tales in the "*Thakurmar Jhuli*" written by DM Majumdar a noted Bengali fairytale writer in India. The seven champa flowers are seven brothers and the flower parul is their only younger sister.

Partha: He is also known as Arjuna. (Hindu myth)

Pashori: A traditional song of north western Indian region including Himachal, and Kashmir.

Pasupata : The name of Shiva's weapon.(Hindu myth)

*Paush: The ninth month of the Bengali calendar year. Winter begins in this month.

(from mid December to mid January)

Peshwaj: Peshwaj is a kind of embroidered stitched garment full of grandeur for the women in high society in Chamba, India.

Pinak-pani: Name of the God Shiva. He is seen as supreme god as well as god of destruction in Hinduism(Hindu myth).

Piran : A long robe.

Piyal: Latin name: *Buchanania lanzan. Piyal*:(Cashew family) medium-sized deciduous tree, growing to about 50 ft tall. Habitat: Eastern part of India and Bangladesh.

Polash: Its botanical name:*Butea monosperma*. Flowers are in bright orange-red. Polash are native to tropical and subtropical parts of the Indian Subcontinent.

Polashi : A name of a field on the bank of Bhagirathi river, India where the battle (On 21 June 1757) took place between the English mercenaries led by Robert Clive of East-India Company and ruling Nawab of Bangla, Bihar and Orissa, Nawab Shiraj-ud-Daulah.

Porshu: A warrior incarnation of the lord Vishnu who carries an axe. (Hindu myth). He is son of Renuka and the saptarishi Jamadagni. He beheaded his mother Renuka by his axe to carry out his father's command.

Poush: The ninth month of Bangla calendar year. It is a month of winter.

Prahlada: An Asura (demon) prince who was very much devoted to Vishnu. He was also a saint amongst infidels(Hindu Myth).

Projapati: Brahma -protector of all living creatures (Hindu Myth).

Pujarini : The term Pujarini means a female devotee who worships Hindu god and goddesses. But here in this poem the Poet describes his beloved as his Pujarini. She is devoted to poet with her love.

Purobi or Purvi: An Indian musical mode (raga).

Qais: The legendary character who met his beloved Laili

after many obstacles and died when he met her.

Rabi: Poet Rabindranath Tagore.

Radhika: The lover of lord Krishna (Hindu myth).

Raga: 'Raga' means musical mode. A particular classical mode of Indian music.

Raga Purobi : An Indian musical mode or raga.

Rajonighanda: In Bengali, it is called "Rajoni-Gandha", meaning "Scent of the Night". It is a garden plant (*Polianthes tuberosa*) of the Amaryllis family which blooms at night with sweet smell.

Rakhi: A piece of thread which one ties round the wrist of another in order to safeguard the latter from evils. It a Hindu tradition.

Rama/Ram: He is seventh avatar of Vishnu and a king of Ayodhya, a place described in ancient Indian puranas[Hindu myth].

Ranchi: A city in India. A mental hospital is situated there for treating patients with mental disorders.

Rangada: A name to call a fair complexioned elder brother instead of calling him by name. 'Ranga' means white complexioned, 'dada' means brother.

Rangadidi: A name to call a fair complexioned elder sister instead of calling her by name. 'Ranga' means white complexioned, 'didi' means sister.

Rangan : Its botanical name is *Ixora coccinea*. It grows in tropical and subtropical areas throughout the world. The plants possess leathery leaves, ranging from 3 to 6 inches in length, and produce large clusters of tiny red flowers in the summer.

Rangmohal: A pleasure house for entertainment built by the Mughal Emperors in India.

Rasatala : It is the lowest of the seven underworlds or the hells. (Hindu myth)

Rati: She is the Hindu goddess of love, carnal desire, lust and passion. Rati is the female counterpart, the chief consort of Kama (Kamadeva), the god of love [Hindu myth].

Ravana: The arch-villain of the Rama, the king of Lanka. He is portrayed as a powerful demon king who disturbs the penances of *Rishis*. Vishnu incarnates as the human Rama to defeat him, thus circumventing the boon given by Brahma. (Hindu Myth).

Rekab: Plates.

Roy-bahadur: The title was offered to the respectable Hindus by the British government in India.

Rubai: Poem with four-lined stanza (quatrains).

Sachi : The wife of Indra (Hindu myth).

Sachi betel leaf: The people of Indian sub-continent chew a kind of smelly leaf known as sachi pan or sachi betel leaf.

Sajne: Latin Name:*Moringa oleifera*. Tree grows upto 12m. It produces cream colored flowers.

Sahnai: An Indian double reeded flute played by blowing air from the mouth. It touches the heart as it creates long sustained mournful lamenting melodic tone when a tearful bride departs her parental home after the wedding ceremonies.

Sahnaiya: The one who plays sahnai.

Salam: The Arabic word salam means peace.

Sankara: The name of Shiva (Hindu Myth).

Sangon: Also Shaon or Shravan, the month of monsoon in Bangladesh.

Saki: A young girl who delivers wine to the wine drinkers in a wine shop.

Sari: Sari is worn by the women of Indian subcontinent. It is a long unstitched cloth draped over the body in various styles. Sari is usually designed and beautified with prints and colors. Its length ranges from five to six yards.

Seunti: A kind of white rose indigenous to Indian sub-continent; another name of shefali.

Shahjahan: His name is Abul Muzaffar Shahabuddin Muhammad Shah Jahan. He was the fifth Mughal Emperor in India from 1628-1658. He built a tomb (Tajmohal) over his wife's graveyard, considered as one of the greatest architectures marveled over other man-made architectures, stands proudly as one of the seventh wonders of the world.

Shampan: A kind of small boat in Bangladesh; both ends are narrow and curved like a crescent moon.

Shahidi-Eid: Eid of martyrs. Eid means festivity.

Shakuntala: She was born of the sage Vishwamitra and apshara Menaka. Rishi Kanva found her in a forest as a baby surrounded by Shakunta birds. Therefore he named her Shakuntala meaning Shakunta-protected (Hindu Myth).

Shal: Latin name: *Shorea robursta*. It is a timber plant grows in Bangladesh and India.

Shakyamuni: Shakyamuni was the son of the king of a

minor Indian kingdom in what is now Nepal. Modern researchers date his life to either about 560-480 BCE or about 460-380 BCE. His father was king of the Shakya tribe, and Shakyamuni means "sage of the Shakyas." He is commonly known by the names Gautama and Siddhartha.

Shampan: A small wooden boat in Bangladesh curved at both ends like a crescent moon.

Shangon: It is also shrabana, the month of incessant rain or ceaseless downpour.

Shanka : In Hinduism the shankha (conch shell) is a sacred emblem of the Hindu preserver god Vishnu. The shankha is still used as a trumpet in Hindu ritual, and as a war trumpet in the past.

Shaontal: An indigenous people live in some parts of Bangladesh and in West Bengal (India). They live mostly in hilly and forest areas of the country.

Sharada : Another name for the Hindu goddess Saraswati. (Hindu Myth.)

Shari : A kind of Bangladshi boat-song.

Sharong: A worker who operates the engine of the ship.

Sharosh: They are the water-birds of Bangladesh live in the vast low lying areas of the country.

Shwaraswati : She is the goddess of knowledge, music, arts and science. She is the consort of Brahma.[Hyndu myth]

Shayma: An Indian cuckoo.

Shayambar: It means self-choice. A bride who chooses a man as her husband from amongst a number of invit'd suitors at a public assembly.

Shefalika/ Shefali: Botanical name: *Nyctanthes arbortristis*. It is commonly known as Night-flowering Jasmine with sweet smell found in abundance in and around Bangladesh. It is also known as Shefali or Sheuli.

Shejo: Third in order of birth; third in order of seniority among brothers, or sisters, or uncles, or aunts, or in-laws.

Sheuli: Also known as *Shefali*, a white colored flower found in Indian

Subcontinent. Its botanical name is *Nyctanthes arbortristis*, commonly known as

Night-flowering Jasmine.

Shimul : Its botanical name is *Bombax ceiba*. In full bloom, the flower is red in color and large with six-inch diameter and consists of five thick, fleshy petals with an oily or satin sheen. The flowers are bright red in color with nectar. They bloom in spring season all over Indian sub-continent.

Shiraji: Hafiz of Shiraz(1326-1390) is widely recognized as the pre-eminent master of Persian ghazal. Shiraji was one of the great sufi poets.

Shirnee: An oblation of food offered to common and poor people on a sacred occasion.

Shish-mohal: The dwelling house or palace made of mirrors and was built by Moghal Emperors in India as a palace of rest and pleasure.

Shita: Wife of king Rama (in myth story of Hindu Ramayana) and daughter of king Janoki. She protected her chastity from Ravana, the king of Lanka, who abducted her.(Hindu myth).

Shelim : The another name of great Mughal Emperor

Jehanghir(1569-1627)

Sherbet: A kind of sweet drink.

Shiraj : A famous 16th century Persian Poet.

Shiri: A character in Arabian story. She dedicated and sacrificed her life for the beloved Farhad.

Shirni: it is a way of feeding the poor or the common people in Indian Muslim community on any sacred occasion with a good intention.

Shiuli: Night-flowering Jasmine, botanical name: *Nyctanthes arbor-tristis*. It is also known as shefali.

Shiva: He is seen as supreme god as well as god of destruction in Hinduism.

Shivajee: (19 February 1627 -3 April 1680) He was the founder of the Maratha Empire, which lasted until 1818. Shivaji led a resistance to free the Maratha people from the Adilshahi Sultanate of Bijapur during the Mughal empire.

Shombhu: A name of a Hindu male.

Shravana: The fourth month of Bangla calendar year. It is the month of monsoon.

Shyam: It is another name for Lord Krishna, narrated in Hindu Vagavat Purana (Hindu myth).

Simum: A typical sand storm in desert.

Sindur: Vermillion used by Hindu married women who put the impression of vermillion on their foreheads.

Sitar: An Indian stringed musical instrument. It is a long-necked lute and is believed to be influenced by the Vina. Its distinctive timbre and resonance create from the sympathetic strings and bridge.

Sithi: The line that is created after parting of hair on the head.

Sorai: A kind of long elongated, curve-nosed water pitcher used by the people of Arabian Peninsula, Persia and Indian sub-continent to drink wine or water.

Sorat/ Shorot: It is the autumn season in Bangladesh. It begins just after the monsoon (Barsha) season.

Suradhuni: The Ganges, the river of god flowing as if from the heaven. (Hindu myth)

Swaraj: A government within the government was introduced ignoring the British rule in India by Mahatma Ghandi. It means self-governance—ruled by the people of the country ignoring the existing government.

Swaraji : The people who followed the idea of self governance are called Swaraji.

Swaraswati : The goddess of knowledge, music and arts. She is the consort of Brahma, also revered as his Shakti. (Hindu Myth.)

Tahura: A kind of heavenly wine.

Tajmohal: It is a white marble mausoleum located in Agra, India. It was built by Mughal Emperor Shahjahan in memory of his third wife, Mumtaz. The Tajmahal was built between the years 1632 to 1648.

Tambul: The raw betel nut (soaked in water) is called 'Tambul' in Assam and the paan is called Tambul paan (betel leaf).

Tiki: A small tuft of hair hangs from the back of clean shaved head of some people of Hindu religious sect.

Tilttoma: A mythological virgin woman of incomparable beauty. (Hindu Myth).

Tip: An impression or dot of any kind of paste of vermilion, saffron etc. on the forehead or cheek applied by finger tips as a mark of sanctity.

Togor : This flower is named as Cape Jasmine. Latin name: *Tabernaemontana coroneria.* The flower smells sweet. It grows in Bangladesh and India.

Tomal: A species of dark colored tree in Eastern part of India and Bangladesh.

Tori : It is a Hindustani classical raga or musical mode- Tori thaat, one of the ten modes of Hindustani classical music.

Uccaisraba: The horse of Indra, the god of thunder (Hindu Myth).

Uma: Another name of Parvati or Durga. She is the consort of shiva (Hindu myth.)

Urbashi: The name of the chief dancer of heaven famous for her ageless youth and undying beauty (Hindu myth.)

Vadar: Also Vadra the fifth month of Bangla calendar year. The month of Barsa or monsoon.

Veda: Veda is the oldest scriptures of Hinduism. It is a philosophical text composed in Vedic Sanskrit.

Vedanta: It means the end goal of Vedas or Upanishads. Is is also a school of philosophy that interpreted the Upanishads.

Veel: They are Adibashi (members of aboriginal people) in north eastern India.

Vishnu : He is the Supreme god in the Vaishnavite tradition of Hinduism [Hindu myth].

Vishwamitra: One of the great sages narrated in Valmiki's Mahabharata(Hindu Myth).

Vishnu: He is the Supreme god in the Vaishnavite tradition of Hinduism. Vishnu is the one one who supports, preserves, sustains and governs the universe.(Hindu myth)

Yaksa: A demon appointed to guard a treasure of King Kuvera[Hindu myth].

Yama: The Hindu god of death[Hindu myth].

Yazid: (23 July 647 - 14 November 683) He was a son of Muawiyah(The second Caliph of Ummayed dynasty). Yazid killed Hussain in an ambush. He was appointed as a Khalifa (Caliph) by his father Muawiyah. He reigned for three years (from 680 AD until his death in 683 AD).

Yobana: A non-Hindu; a Muslim.

Yogi: An ascetic -the one who meditates in seclusion.

Yudhistira: He was a king. He was a warrior who fought with spear while riding *ratha or* chariot (Hindu myth).

Zainul Abedin: He was the son of Imam *Hussain*. (See Hassan)

Zakat: It is an obligatory charity (2.5%) for all Muslims to be paid to the poor from one's surplus annual income. The Arabic word zakat derives from the verb zaka, meaning to grow, to increase and to purify.

*Zoglul: Saad Zaghul, Sa'd Zaghloul Pasha ibn Ibrahim) (1859 - August 23, 1927) was an Egyptian revolutionary, and statesman. He was the Prime Minister of Egypt from January 26, 1924 to November 24, 1924.

Zohora: Originated from Arabic word Zahra. It is usually a feminine name.

Dictionaries and Encyclopaedia consulted:

1. Samsad Bengali-English dictionary. 3rd ed. Calcutta, Sahitya Samsad, 2000.
2. Bengali-English dictionary- BanglaAcademy, Dhaka, Bangladesh 29th reprint 2011.
3. Student's Favourite Dictionary (Bengali to English.) by A.T. Dev edition: august 2008.
4. Oxford English Dictionary.
5. Roget's International Thesaurus.
6. Funk& Wagnalls Desk Standard Dictionary.
7. Encyclopaedia Britanica

THE END

Lightning Source UK Ltd.
Milton Keynes UK
UKHW010635170719
346320UK00001B/31/P